What's a Mother to Do?

What's a Mother to Do?

Ann Edwards Cannon

For Enid,
Enjoy!
Ann Edwards Cannon

Signature Books   •   Salt Lake City

∞ *What's a Mother to Do?* was printed on acid-free paper
and was composed, printed, and bound in the United States.

© 1997 by Ann Edwards Cannon
Signature Books is a registered trademark of Signature Books, Inc.

2001   2000   99   98   97   5   4   3   2   1

Library of Congress Cataloging-in-Publication Data
What's a mother to do? / by Ann Edwards Cannon.
     p.   cm.
    ISBN 1-56085-095-7 (pbk. : alk. paper)
     1. American wit and humor.   I. Title.
PN6162.V26   1997
814'.54—dc21   97-28908
                                               CIP

This book is dedicated to my mother

Patti Louise Covey Edwards

a woman of

rare graciousness, generosity, and good humor.

Patti Louise Covey

Contents

Acknowledgements

I wish to thank those persons who, over the past ten years, have made these essays possible: Karen Hale and Jeanne Jardine, owners and editors of *Parent Express*; Keith and Maryjane Whisenant, owners and publishers of *This People* magazine; Bill Smart, Maurine and Scot Proctor, and Jim Bell, editors of *This People* magazine; and most especially Patty Kimball, founder of *Parent Express*, who started the whole thing.

*You Say Tomato: The Real
Difference between Men
and Women*

The Real Difference
between Men and Women

I read an article in the newspaper the other night that talked about the differences between men and women. The article dealt primarily with differences in social behavior, the kinds of little differences that might crop up at mixed dinner parties where everyone has to figure out how to use more than one fork. According to this article, certain persons with Ph.D.s in psychology have discovered that men interrupt women about ten-to-the-47th power times more often than women interrupt men. That's why when men and women are together at dinner parties you might hear a conversation like this:

WOMAN: The other day when I was downtown I ran into—
MAN: Yo Honey! Pass me the dip!

These same psychologists who discovered that men interrupt women also claim that men are more assertive than women when it comes to expressing themselves. A man dying of starvation, for instance, will always say, "I'm dying of starvation," whereas a woman likewise dying of starvation will murmur politely, "Is anybody here hungry? Can I get anybody something to eat?"

My own mother used to talk a little like this when we were teenagers. When she'd say, "Would anybody here like a Snickers bar?" what she really meant was, "Get some money from your father and go buy me a Snickers bar." But I digress.

I thought the article was interesting as far as it went, but it left out the crucial difference between the sexes which, in my opinion, is that a woman will ALWAYS stop to ask for directions and a man NEVER will. I happen to know this is true because I have lived with men all my life—first my father and brothers and now my husband. All of them are honorable, decent, sensitive men who hardly ever interrupt my mother and me, and yet all of them, it seems, would rather spend their time getting on and off the same freeway interchange fifty times than stopping to ask for directions. I really think we spent half of our family vacations to Los Angeles sitting in a station wagon while my dad and brothers tried to figure out how to get us from my Aunt Alta's apartment to Dodger Stadium without asking anybody for directions along the way.

My husband, Ken, is no different from any other man in my family. Once when the two of us were travelling home through Colorado, we accidentally ended up in Durango otherwise known as the "Pinto Bean Capital of the World." We wound up in Durango because Ken made a wrong turn somewhere between Colorado Springs and Grand Junction and he wouldn't listen to me when I said I thought we were going the wrong way and didn't he want to pull into the next gas station to find out for sure. The reason I knew we were going the wrong way was because I had already been to Durango once before with my own father who was probably on his way to some place else, too.

When I was teaching freshman English at Brigham Young University, I mentioned that if my female-being-lost-in-a-car-with-a-guy-who-refuses-to-stop-for-directions story is such a universal experience, then the Ancient Greeks must have written myths about it. Anyway when I asked my male students why they refused to get directions, they all puffed out their chests and informed me that they never ask for directions because THEY'RE NEVER REALLY LOST IN THE FIRST PLACE! For guys it's just a matter of time. They know that if they drive down every street in America they will eventually find the place they are looking for without having to stop and admit to a complete stranger that they have no idea what planet they're on let alone in which part of town.

My friend Cindy thinks this is the real reason why men refuse to stop. They hate to look stupid in front of other men who work at really macho places like gas stations and Circle K stores. So they just go ahead and drive around in circles all day which is clearly the manly thing to do.

My husband, Ken, now concedes that driving around in hopes that he'll eventually stumble onto the place he wants to be is not a very efficient use of his time. He still won't stop for directions, however. Instead, he's taken to handing me a map and asking me to navigate. This would work out great if only I could figure out how to read a map. However, I missed that day in school when they had the lecture called "MAPS AND HOW TO READ ONE." I also missed the days when they mentioned decimals and why we need them, as well as how many pints really do equal one quart.

So if you see a married couple driving up and down, up and down your street and you notice that the woman is holding a map wrong side up, you'll know it's only Ken and me.

We're just trying to find our way home from Durango.

The Real Difference
between Men and Women, Part II

*L*ately I've been musing on yet another difference between men and women—i.e., their responses to maneuvering extremely large vehicles in tight quarters. I started thinking about this the other day when Ken asked me to assist him in parallel parking a big truck of the U-Haul variety. I was supposed to (a) direct while he (b) drove.

Of course I started to panic and perspire all over the place because I knew from direct personal experience what would happen:

1. He would tell me what to do.
2. I would try to do it.
3. He would tell me I was doing it wrong.
4. I would tell him to take a hike and perhaps make a rude gesture or two.
5. He would yell at me and before you know it, we'd be fighting in front of all the neighbors just like a couple of crazy teenagers in love.

This kind of fight happens because Ken is a guy whereas I definitely am not, which means that we simply do not speak the same language. For example, when I stand there on the curb and say, "You're fine, Sweetheart, except you're getting kind of close," I think I have done a masterful job of summing up the situation—i.e., that he is fine because he hasn't rammed into the neighbor's pickup although give or take a few inches and he will. Also I think the whole "Sweetheart" thing is a nice touch. It shows him how supportive I am, don't you know.

So what does he do? He slams on the brakes and bangs his forehead against the windshield just like my dad did that day I got my learner's permit.

Dad and I were taking a little test drive to the grocery store to return a vast quantity of empty Coke bottles. As I approached an intersection whose light had just turned yellow, I began to accelerate with the intent of leaving the Gremlin next to me in the dust.

Dad roared at me. "Stop!"

I'll tell you the truth. I was torn. On the one hand, I really wanted to obey my father, the man who'd given me life and so forth. On the other hand, I hated to think that I was the kind of girl who could be beaten by a Gremlin—a Gremlin, for petessakes—which I used to think was the equivalent of car vermin when I was a young and snotty girl adolescent. So I kept on pressing the gas pedal in a general downward direction.

"STOP!" Dad yelled again.

I fought with myself a second longer, and then I did the thing I thought would best please ye olde fathere. I brought the car to a swift and sudden stop—in the middle of the intersection. To this day I can still see my father pitching forward as if in slow motion, with a thousand empty Coke bottles soaring past his ears.

"WHY DID YOU STOP?" He sounded just like a man who's taken one too many Coke bottles in the head.

"Because you told me to," I said, flipping my hair a little and wondering if I should use some more Sun-In. I almost added a "Duh, Dad," but refrained since I perceived he was somewhat shaken.

At that point my father, who rarely raises his voice, let me have it, which taught me a very important lesson—it's no good trying to please the men in your life, so you just ought to go ahead and please yourself.

But I digress.

As I was saying, when Ken asked me to help him with the U-Haul, I began to hyperventilate—until I had the totally brilliant idea of finding Ken another guy to help him. I imposed upon a neighbor we barely know who graciously agreed to lend a hand.

Now here comes the truly amazing part of my story. Even though our neighbor, Andy, and Ken are barely acquainted with each other, they had this instant non-verbal communication thing going about the truck. Andy stood on the curb and began flapping his arms around like he was trying out for head cheerleader AND KEN ACTUALLY UNDERSTOOD WHAT ANDY MEANT. He parked the U-Haul easily. No problemo, in fact.

"How did you know what Andy meant when he starting doing all that stuff with his hands?" I asked later that evening.

Ken shrugged.

"Did you have to take a special class when we were in junior high school?" I asked. When Ken and I were in junior high school during the Dark Ages, girls and guys used to be separated for certain subjects—Home Economics for girls, Shop for guys; Advanced Note Writing for girls, Arm Language for guys.

Again Ken shrugged which I took to mean he didn't know, although I could be completely wrong.

With guys, I've learned, it can be pretty hard to tell.

How Guys Impress Girls: The Formative Years

As the mother of five sons, I certainly have a unique opportunity to observe emerging Guy Behavior on a regular basis. This once again became very apparent to me the last time I took my kids to Children's Bingo Night.

I used to think you had to (a) be a friend of my grandmother's and (b) have a large strap of your foundation garment showing before they allowed you to participate in the noble sport of Bingo, but here in the New York community where we've been living for the past year, it is a Game for the Young. Here's how Children's Bingo Night works. First, the kids all sit down and eat a meal with real silverware and napkins after which they retire to the game room for a fine session of brisk number calling.

It was the dinner part where I observed one of my children turn into a real Guy.

My two oldest boys quickly found themselves places at a Boys Only type table. No problemo there. I knew they'd feel right at home listening to everyone's stories about skiing off twenty-foot moguls and so forth.

My sweet, dreamy eight-year-old didn't fare so well. By the time he realized it was Wednesday again, and he was actually at Bingo Night, all the guy seats were taken—the only room left was at a table FULL OF GIRLS.

Miserable to the core, he slid carefully into his seat, trying very hard not to (a) make physical contact with or (b) breathe the same air as any girl persons. Yes, it was a sad and joyless son, a glum and downcast son, a morose and heavy-hearted son I saw before me. To be the only eight-year-old boy cast adrift in a roiling sea full of females is a hard thing indeed.

About half way through dinner, however, the most amazing thing happened. My son looked up from his bar-b-que ribs long enough to make accidental eye contact with the very fine looking little girl sitting next to him. Maybe it was her thick dark hair pulled back in a casual pony tail. Maybe it was her bright red cheeks. Maybe it was the way she sneered at him. Whatever it was, my son was hooked. I watched it happen. Lightning had struck. The next thing I knew, he was doing his level best to impress her.

First, he tried making various disgusting noises such as (a) dying frog sounds and (b) burps, which is something his oldest brother once earned a merit badge for at Scout Camp.

She was unmoved.

Then he picked up a paper cup and stuffed it in his mouth, after which he slowly chewed it to a papery pulp without taking his eyes off her once.

Her indifference was monumental.

Finally, in a fit of desperation, he picked up his fork AND STARTED COMBING HIS HAIR WITH IT.

This finally had the desired effect. She started looking at my son all right—with a look of complete and total horror. Then she elbowed all her little friends, telling them to take a look, too. You would have thought they were all looking at one of those two-headed calves you used to see at the state fair carnival when I was a little girl.

"I can't watch any more of this," I said to one of the fathers sitting next to me. "My son—flesh of my flesh, light of my life, fruit of my loins and so forth—is combing his hair with a fork in public."

The father put down his newspaper and assessed the situation for himself.

"Indeed he is," he said.

"He thinks he's impressing girls," I said.

"True," he agreed. "Combing your hair with a fork is a time-honored mating ritual for males his age. Sort of like showing a cute girl that your mouth is full of mashed potatoes at lunch time."

When I was in elementary school, I had this friend who looked just like Sandra Dee in *Gidget*, and boys were always showing her that their mouths were full of mashed potatoes at lunch time. Also they used to throw spit wads at her on the bus, so I knew exactly what this father was talking about.

"Have you ever noticed," he went on thoughtfully, "that men sometimes have strange notions about what will impress a woman?"

"Well, I'm sure women have odd ideas about what impresses a man, too," I said.

He sighed. "You say tomäto. We say tomato. It's a wonder that our two species ever communicate."

"I know," I agreed. "It's just like talking to the dolphins."

He stared at me like I had suddenly seized my dinner fork and was busy combing my hair with it.

"You know how scientists spend all that time trying to figure out how to talk to dolphins because dolphins talk to each other in code?" I explained. "Well, it's *exactly* like men and women."

Guys.

Sometimes you have to hold up cue cards with great big letters, don't you know.

The True Reason Why Guys Have Been in Charge of the World

*U*p until now I have been confused about a particular issue, namely why men have been the ones in charge of the world. It's not that I don't like men. Some of my best friends are men. In fact, as I have pointed out to friends and family before, I even married one. It's just that I've never exactly understood why we would entrust serious matters such as national security to individuals who refuse to stop and ask for directions when they're lost.

For a while I thought I'd never learn the answer to this question, that it would remain a puzzle to me just like certain other cosmic mysteries such as why I *always* pick the slowest moving line at the grocery store. This happened to me again the other day, as a matter of fact, when I stopped at Albertson's on the way to a wedding in order to buy a pair of nylons, preferably without runs in them. I was in a hurry, so I picked what *appeared* to be the shortest line. There was one well-groomed woman in it, buying a single box of Kix. The checker rang the order up and announced the price.

"Wait a minute," said the well-groomed woman with the Kix. "I think I actually may have clipped a coupon for this."

Even now, as I write, I feel compelled to let out one of those bitter snorts you're always reading about. Shortest line? Ha! The well-groomed women with the Kix pulled out a wad of coupons as thick as your hand from her very expensive Daytimer and began going through them one by one. Now ordinarily I am filled with a respect bordering on awe for people who do coupons since I myself can never find any scissors with which to clip in our house, but this time I thought I'd lose my mind since the couple whose wedding I was supposed to attend got married and had a couple of kids who were well on their way to puberty while I waited for this women to locate her Kix coupon.

"Excuse me," I finally said, "but just exactly how big of a savings are we talking here? Fifteen cents? A quarter? How about if I give you the money SO YOU'LL JUST BUY THOSE KIX AND GO AWAY?"

She didn't answer me, no doubt because I was a stranger ranting right there in the middle of Albertson's with no pantyhose on. Also I was being so incredibly snotty you'd have thought I was in junior high school again. In retrospect, of course, I'm deeply ashamed of myself, and I live in terror that one day she and I will meet again socially because our children will grow up and marry each other. But I digress.

As I was saying, I used to spend a lot of time wondering why guys have been the ones in charge until this spring when the answer became perfectly clear to me. My husband, Ken, and I were at Dylan's kindergarten graduation program which featured the children performing. Basically, this is what happened:

The little girls totally upstaged the little boys.

The little girls knew all the words and all the hand motions and all the dance steps, while the little boys just stood there looking like they'd gotten off at the wrong bus stop.

Half way through the program, one of the little girls turned around and actually started mouthing the words to my son, Dylan, who was too busy watching a fly to notice that she was trying to help him along.

This isn't the first time I've noticed the fact that little girls are much more advanced than little boys. My friend's girl baby, for instance, can practically buy her own shoes on sale, let alone put them on, whereas my boy baby, who is exactly the same age, still thinks that shoes are something you stuff in your mouth.

"Have you ever noticed how girls seem to develop faster than boys?" I asked Ken on the way home from Dylan's program.

"Are you kidding?" he said. "I was the only male in a family full of sisters. They did everything better than I did. So did the girls at school."

"Speaking of girls doing things better than boys, did I ever tell you that I once beat Jose deHoyos in the fifty-yard dash when we were in the sixth grade?"

Jose deHoyos was the fastest boy in the entire school and I whipped him one day at recess even though I was wearing a dress and he wasn't. To this day, beating Jose still rates as one of my favorite life memories.

Ken sighed. "See what I mean?"

"So what happened?" I asked. "How did guys grow up to be the ones in charge?"

"Well," said Ken philosophically, "boys catch up with girls eventually, and when they do, frankly, they're pretty mad about all those years they spent looking like dorks in kindergarten programs and so forth. They get even by refusing to cut women in on the adult action."

"That's not fair," I pointed out.

"Very true," he agreed, "which is why things are changing."

"Well," I huffed, "I'm certainly all for change."

And I am, too, although I don't believe for a second that the little girls will stop showing up the little boys in the near future.

Some things will always stay the same.

Real Men Don't Have Babies

I think it's high time we re-establish a crucial fact that our very advanced society has totally lost sight of—i.e., which sex actually gives birth.

Back in the Middle Ages people were very clear on this point. They may have mistakenly believed that the moon was made of cheese and that flossing regularly after meals made your teeth fall out, but there was no doubt in their minds that the women—not the men—were the ones having the babies. Even as little as twenty-five years ago, the general American public could be counted on to answer the following multiple choice question correctly:

QUESTION: Who has the babies?
    a. Men
    b. Women

Everybody knew the answer was b., of course, because they'd all seen enough 1950s-style sitcoms to know that it was the woman's job to say, "I think the baby is coming, Dear," while it was clearly the man's job to spring out of his twin bed, eyeballs spinning like cherries in a slot machine, and scream, "My wife is having a booby! I mean she's having a baby!" before accidentally locking himself in the bedroom closet.

That, however, was B.D.—"Before Donahue"—who showed up on national television one day carrying a mike and wearing a skirt and encouraging men to show their sensitive sides.

Nothing has been the same since.

One of the ways that men started showing their sensitive sides was to get more involved in the whole birthing process from pregnancy to delivery. When my parents were having their children, for instance, all that was required of my dad was to drive my mom to the hospital, park the car, then read back issues of *Sports Illustrated* with all the other expectant fathers in the waiting room.

Now, however, enlightened men like my husband, Ken, go to prenatal classes so that they can learn how to bathe and change plastic dolls, which comes in very handy later on if their wives happen to give birth to a Barbie. Men also learn in prenatal class how to "coach" their wives through childbirth which incidentally isn't supposed to hurt very much if you just figure out how to breathe right.

Well, I don't mind men getting involved in the childbirth deal except for one little thing. They're starting to get the idea that they're really the ones doing all the work—timing contractions, reminding you to breathe through your mouth instead of your nose, fetching ice chips—while you're just lying there in a comfortable bed whining and otherwise being in a bad mood.

Actually, I've noticed that men do this sort of thing quite often. While I happen to like and respect men very much—I even married one—they do have this tendency to think that everything they do is somehow bigger and more significant than everything you do. They work harder, they play harder, they suffer harder, especially if they happen to have the flu or a cold. Most men really do believe in their heart of hearts that they are more miserable than their wives when both of them get sick at the same time.

They figure this is true because their wives keep rolling out of bed to make lunch for everybody which everybody knows they couldn't possibly do if they were really ill.

The reason I bring this all up is that I am going to have another baby, and I truly hope that the same thing that happened to me the first time I had a baby doesn't happen again.

I'd had a long and difficult labor—I'm sure because I wasn't breathing right—during which Ken never once left my side. He was, in short, the model "birthing partner," encouraging me, making me as comfortable as possible, talking me through contractions. When I finally had the baby, the medical staff cheered and ran around the delivery room, whooping loudly and giving each other high fives. Then they congratulated Ken on how brilliantly he had coached me through the whole thing after which they hoisted him on their shoulders and carried him off to the locker room. The only thing anybody said to me was would I please turn off the lights when I left. I'm sorry but I just didn't think that was exactly fair. So what if I wasn't the guy with the headphones calling the plays? At least I was there. I contributed.

Hey! I even have a kid to prove it!

How Not to Act When Your Husband Gets a Speeding Ticket

I may not have been the world's best Driver's Ed. student in high school—the word brilliant, for example, was seldom the word of choice on most of my classmates' lips—but I did learn the following important lesson: DO NOT UNDER ANY CIRCUMSTANCES TRUST YOUR BEST FRIEND, GIGI BALLIF, WHEN SHE'S BEHIND THE WHEEL OF A DRIVER'S ED. CAR.

This is what happened. Gigi and I were assigned to the same car on the driving range, which meant that she and I were supposed to take turns behind the wheel—stopping and starting, backing up, parallel parking, maneuvering through cones, and generally avoiding cars driven by boys in the class, all of whom thought they were actually on the bumper car ride at Lagoon Amusement Park.

It was an awesome responsibility, don't you know.

Anyway, after a few moments of sitting in the car, preparing ourselves mentally for the challenges that lay ahead, Gigi (who was behind the wheel) finally turned on the engine and popped the car into gear. But whereas I was naively expecting to *back away* from the curb, we actually *leaped forward* onto the grass, sort of like a rabbit whose nerves are on edge, and began felling objects in front of us.

Gigi screamed. I screamed. Mr. Moon, the Driver's Ed. teacher, did a rain dance on the blacktop. We took out a tree of the young sapling variety. The car screeched to a stop. We shook.

"This reminds me of that time we almost drove your father's golf cart into the lake," I pointed out.

But that's another story.

So that was the big lesson I learned in Driver's Ed., which frankly hasn't been that useful to me as an adult since Gigi rarely runs into trees these days. Also all that time I spent in the simulator wasn't very useful in my real life either since I've discovered you can't carpool your kids in one.

What I would have appreciated more is some specific instruction on how to respond appropriately when your husband—the Love of Your Life, the Light in Your Eyes, the Song in Your Heart, the Spring in Your Step, and so on—gets a speeding ticket. Mr. Moon could have even made a multiple choice question out of it.

> QUESTION: Which of the following comments would be inappropriate to make to your husband when he is pulled over by an officer of the law?
> a. I always thought you were a b-b brain.
> b. How come you are such a b-b brain?
> c. The cop is a b-b brain and so are you.

Naturally, I would never call my husband, Ken, a b-b brain because, as our ten-year-old son has pointed out, his father is even smarter than Alex Trebeck. Not only that, but Ken rarely gets tickets of any kind, whereas I manage to collect a parking ticket or two every time I leave the house. Ken prides himself on not getting tickets. It's sort of a point of honor with him in the way these things are to men. Not that he hasn't deserved a few here and there. It's just that Heaven, as it were, has been kind.

Lady Luck, however, was not with him that fateful day on Interstate 70. We were just outside of Independence, Missouri, when we saw lights flashing behind us.

"Pull over," I said to Ken. "You were speeding."

Ken took umbrage. "I was not speeding. I'm going uphill in a family car hauling five kids, six basketballs, a luggage rack and several hundred pounds of Gameboy gear. How could I possibly be speeding? *It's not aerodynamically possible.*"

By now his face was red and the muscles in his neck were standing out for all the world to see.

In retrospect, I know I should have handled things differently. I should have railed at the fates with Ken by (a) beating my breast, (b) heaping ashes all over my head, (c) rending my clothes, (d) rending his clothes, and (e) so forth.

Or I should have just kept my mouth shut. I hear keeping one's mouth shut is a very good idea sometimes. But no. I couldn't help myself.

I started to laugh.

I laughed as the officer, decked out in Standard Issue Southern

Lawman Sunglasses, walked to our car. I laughed as he poked his head inside our window and told us how fast we'd been going. I laughed when he asked for Ken's license. You would have thought I was the world's happiest gal, I was just laughing so much.

"Is he giving you a ticket, Dad?" one of the boys asked.

Kids. They love to be kept current on this sort of thing.

I laughed some more.

Not too long ago when Ken and I were talking about our little trip through the great state of Missouri, he said, "Sometimes you laugh at the oddest moments."

"It's true," I said. "I'm sure it makes friends and family nervous whenever they have to trot me out in public. Who knows when I'll start up again. Have you paid that ticket, by the way?"

He gave a resigned nod.

"Do you mind if I write about it?" I asked.

He thought for a minute, then said, "Only if you make one thing perfectly clear."

"Yes?"

"I wasn't really speeding."

I didn't even crack a smile.

Telephone Trauma

*O*n paper, at least, the whole idea of communication seems so simple. Here's how it's supposed to work: Person A talks while Person B listens. Then Person A listens while Person B talks. At the end of this exchange both of them know exactly what the other one is thinking.

The whole thing's a snap.

Of course this process never works smoothly in real life because such factors as (a) age and (b) sex get in the way.

Age, of course, can be a significant barrier to effective communication, especially if you are dealing with individuals much younger than yourself. I've learned from direct personal experience, for example, that you can talk to a baby until you are totally blue in the face, but in the end he'll only grin, then stick one of his fingers in your eye.

Older children aren't much better. In spite of what you see on *Leave It to Beaver* reruns all the time, it's very difficult to have a conversation with them, let alone one in which you actually get to pass along a Value. For example, whereas a conversation between Ward and the Beav would proceed something like this—

WARD: Do you understand now why it was wrong for you to tell Mrs. Miller that you weren't responsible for breaking her window?

THE BEAV: Sure, Dad. I guess I just wasn't using the old noggin.

—the same conversation at our house would sound more like this—

ME: Do you understand now why it was wrong for you to tell Mrs. Miller that you weren't responsible for breaking her window?

MY KID: Hey, Mom, can we check out a video tonight?

One of the biggest hindrances to communication is the whole male/female thing. Men and women may use the same words all right, but they most certainly do not mean the same things by them. Indeed, we have a little story in our family that vividly illustrates this point.

When my parents were first married, they very stupidly decided not to give each other A SINGLE THING for Christmas so they could save a little money. Of course, what my mother figured this actually meant is that she would scrimp and save and dip heavily into the grocery fund to buy my father manly sweaters and colognes to surprise him with on Christmas morning. She, on the other hand, fully expected him to run out just like that girl in *The Gift of the Magi* and cut off all his hair so he could afford to buy her something useless but sweet in return.

My father, being of the male persuasion, had a slightly different interpretation of the whole situation. He wanted to give my mother a gift, it's true, but since they'd both *said* in plain American English they weren't going to give one another presents, he'd better buck up and do the honorable thing by observing his end of the bargain. Well, naturally you can imagine what a fiasco Christmas was when my mother woke up and realized to her complete horror that *my father still had all his own hair!* You can, I'm sure, figure out the rest of the story on your own.

"Men are fine with the text," she now says. "It's just the subtext they have trouble with."

Of course, a surefire way to screw up the communication process for me personally is to introduce technology of any kind, including the telephone. I really, really hate my telephone. People I don't know are always calling me up at dinnertime, asking me if I want to buy (a) light bulbs and (b) tickets to charity magic shows. At least I get to talk to real human beings in these cases. What really fries me is when someone has their *computer* call me, offering me good deals on condo time shares and so forth. Apparently I have made a big enough stink about this that my children now think that computerized telephone solicitations of any kind are evil and that they should hang up and flee the room the minute they receive one.

This belief, in fact, was the cause of our family's latest Telephone Trauma.

I was in Ogden and desperately needed to touch base with my babysitter at home. I followed the instructions on the pay phone to place a collect call and discovered that sometime in the last decade this entire process has been mechanized so that a recording asks the party at home whether or not they will accept the charge. Unfortunately, for me, my kids—not the babysitter—kept (a) answering the phone and (b) hanging it up before I could talk to them. Finally I got through to a real live operator and asked her to place the call for me because my kids at home just didn't get it. Philip answered when she called.

"Will you accept a long distance call from Ann Cannon?" the operator asked him.

"She isn't here right now," he told her.

Meanwhile I started shouting in the background over the operator's polite, measured tones. "JUST SAY YES, PHILIP! JUST SAY YES!"

The operator, sensing my mounting hysteria, tried a different approach. "Would you like to talk to your mother?"

That's when Philip—my first-born child, flesh of my flesh, light of my life and so on—paused, then answered, "Not really."

Well, I should have known we were not destined to communicate that afternoon: he's young, I'm old; he's a guy, I'm a girl; he says tomato, I say tomäto; we were on a telephone.

Need I say more?

Gotcha : The Kids

Gotcha!

*T*his happened when Philip was four years old.

I was fixing dinner one night when he wandered into the kitchen with my old dog Bogie, who was panting hard in an effort to make me believe he'd been running marathons instead of watching *Divorce Court* all afternoon.

"You wanna play a game?" Philip asked me.

"What kind of a game?" I returned, all primed to fake a faint if the words *Candyland* or *Chutes and Ladders* should tumble from his youthful lips.

"You know," he said, "a Pretend Game. Let's say, like, I'm somebody different and you're somebody different and Bogie's somebody different."

Better than *Candyland* any day, I think you'll agree. "Sure," I said. "Why not?"

Philip bustled about, making up rules and assigning roles. "Say, like, I'm the Man and you're the Kid and Bogie's the Mom."

I looked doubtfully at Bogie who was padding toward the fridge. Bogie as "Utah Young Mother of the Year"? Frankly, I couldn't see it. For one thing he loathes children. For another he doesn't do aerobics or volunteer to teach in language labs for the PTA. Besides, he smells bad on warm days.

But Philip insisted and so our roles were assigned. I was the Kid. Philip was the Man. Bogie was the Mom.

We bantered back and forth in character for a while when Philip started eyeing Bogie carefully. "Hey Kid," he finally said to me in his Man's Voice. "Did you know your Mom looks like a dog?"

I should have seen it coming, but I didn't. I was blind-sided. Conned. Set up by a four-year-old and a duplicitous dog. Talk about your Fagins and your Artful Dodgers.

I've decided that kids are actually rather good at making adults feel foolish. It's their way of evening things up between them and us. The simple fact is that children are horribly, appallingly dependent on grownups for just about everything—food, love, shelter, moral guidance, slurpees at 7-Eleven. They know how much they need us and they resent that need. So they devise all sorts of ways to take us down a few notches, to throw us off balance, to make us stare in a mirror every so often and say, "How now, you Chump."

How else can you explain their awful jokes?

I'm not talking about knock-knock jokes here, however horrible they may be. At least knock-knock jokes make sense, and if you're feeling kindly toward the little poppet who told you the joke, you can fake a loud guffaw and slap your knee at the punchline. No. I'm talking about the jokes kids make up as they go along. (EXAMPLE: Why did the dragon cross the road? Because he was really a dinosaur!) These kinds of jokes don't make sense and they aren't funny, not even if you've had too much gas at the dentist's office. But kids love them. They squeal like little gnomes at one another's jokes, while you, the Big Person, stare stupidly into space. Gotcha, they say.

Kids lie for much the same reason. They like to watch you scramble when their friends go to you to verify a story. I frequently have neighbor children ask me things like, "Is it true Philip is a ninja?" or "Is it true that Alec rode an ostrich?" If I say no, Philip is not a ninja, then I run the risk of embarrassing him in front of his peers. But if I say yes, I run the risk of neighbor children telling their parents that Ann says yes it's true Philip used to live in China and yes it's true Alec's grandfather is a wizard. Gotcha again.

And even though they are supposed to be teetering on the brink of adulthood, adolescents love to one-up us, too. Take what happened to me the other night when I went by myself to a local hamburger drive-in. A teenaged girl, chewing her gum and chipping old polish from her nails, stopped dreaming about appearing on *Star Search* long enough to take my order. Since I was ordering for half the neighborhood as well as for my own family and a few Eastern Bloc track and field teams, it was a large order to be sure. "Twenty burgers, fourteen fries, sixteen onion rings, fry sauce, all the caramel shakes you have on tap, and a Diet Coke with lemon, please," I told her.

She dutifully wrote this information down, repeated it back, checked the car to make sure I was alone, then glued her eyes upon me and asked with a perfectly straight face, "Is this order to stay or to go?"

Side-swiped again.

I've thought about fighting back, but I know it's no use. The kids will just change the rules or the punchline or the tall tale on me. So I guess I'll have to get used to playing Rowan to their Martin, Abbott to their Costello, Hardy to their Laurel. It's not an entirely bad life, I guess.

Especially for someone whose mom looks like a dog.

How to Fight Like a Five-Year-Old

So there I was in front of the YWCA, waist deep in slush, juggling a baby on one hip and a fifty-ton diaper bag on the other, trying to convince my five-year-old son to follow me inside.

ME: You'll have fun.

DYLAN: I don't want to go today.

ME: Come on, Sweetheart. Let's cooperate.

DYLAN: Where's my turtle blimp?

ME: At home on your shelf. Please come inside with me. I'm geting cold, and I'll bet you're getting cold, too.

DYLAN: I WANT MY TURTLE BLIMP!

ME (wondering why an intelligent person like myself is having a conversation about turtle blimps in public): Dylan, please—

DYLAN: I HATE PLEASE! (Falls on the ground and screams loudly so that people walking by will be sure to think that his mother is abusing him.)

Normally at that point I would have tucked Dylan beneath my arm like a football and carried him through the door, only I didn't have any arms—sort of like that time in high school when I played donkey basketball.

(DONKEY BASKETBALL: A variety of basketball in which both teams try to make shots while mounted on donkeys who trot up and down the court looking for spectators to trample.)

Playing donkey basketball was like having no arms because I was hanging on for dear life every time somebody threw me the ball which meant that I kept getting hit in the head.

I'm sure you've all had a similar experience.

Anyway, Dylan wouldn't budge. Not only that but my arms were going into extreme shock thanks to the baby who was (a) eating my hair and (b) putting his fingers in my ear, so I lost it right there in front of the Y.

ME: If you don't come with me right now, I'm going to sneak into your room tonight and THROW ALL YOUR NINJA TURTLES STRAIGHT OUT THE WINDOW!
DYLAN: Uh-uh!
ME: Uh-huh!
DYLAN: Okay fine then I'll just lock my door.
ME: Okay fine then I'll just break it down with my numchuks.
DYLAN: UH-UH!
ME: UH-HUH!
DYLAN (sticking his tongue out): You're so mean.
ME (sticking my tongue out): I know you are but what am I?

At this point Dylan knew he'd been whipped, so he surrendered and followed me meekly inside.

For awhile I felt very guilty about being reduced to a five-year-old's level, but then a new thought occurred to me: generally speaking, we parents try to behave like adults when handling differences with our children which is actually pretty stupid of us because kids have never been adults themselves and therefore have no idea what we're talking about. For this reason, I've decided that if you want to win arguments with your children, you have to fight like they do.

The following is a handy guide that explains how to fight like a kid of any age.

How to Fight Like a Toddler

If you want to fight like a two-year-old, be sure to scream NO a lot and throw stuff, especially food.

How to Fight Like a Grade School Kid

A very useful tactic is to echo whatever your adversary says because it ultimately drives them mad. Here's how it works:

CHILD: I don't want to clean my bedroom.
YOU: I don't want to clean my bedroom.
CHILD: Mom, quit it!
YOU: Mom, quit it,
CHILD: Copy-cat.
YOU: Copy-cat.

How to Fight Like a Fourteen-year-old Girl

No doubt about it. Fighting like a fourteen-year-old girl requires a lot of emotional energy. It can be done, however, as the following conversation demonstrates.

> TEEN: Mom, I don't want to practice the piano.
>
> YOU (whining): But all the other mothers' daughters practice the piano!
>
> TEEN: Mom—
>
> YOU: YOU DON'T UNDERSTAND! NOBODY UNDER-STANDS! (Dissolve into tears, run to your bedroom and slam the door, then pick up the telephone and call [a] your best friend or [b] a boy you met at the mall yesterday.)

You'll notice that I don't give any pointers on how to fight like a baby. That's because babies don't fight. They just sit there drooling and pulling off their socks and being totally charming in a wet kind of way and, before you know it, you're hooked for good which is why you put up with them for the rest of their lives.

Babies are pretty darn sneaky if you ask me.

Playing Games

*T*here it was, nearly 500 degrees in the shade, and I was playing tennis in the middle of a summer afternoon with my seven-year-old son, Alec, because I was trying to be a Good Mother.

"Okay, your serve," I called to him gamely. Alec promptly lobbed his ball into the center of the net. "Fifteen-Love!" he screamed. "I'm totally wasting you, Mom."

"Wait a minute here, Sweetheart," I said. "The ball didn't go over the net. It's my point."

He snorted. "Yeah right."

So that's how things went with us. Alec kept hitting the ball into the net and giving himself points for it, and in the end I lost. Big.

"Geez," Alec said as we crawled into our car to leave. "You kind of stink at tennis."

That's when I came up with another of my little Rules for Living: NEVER PLAY GAMES WITH A PERSON UNDER FOUR FEET TALL.

I really hate playing stuff with kids for a number of reasons—the main one being that they're always changing the rules on you. Take the way we play *Candyland* at our house for instance.

Official Rules for Playing *Candyland* with the Cannons
1. Have a big fight over which color of gingerbread boy you get.
2. Line up gingerbread boys at the starting point.
3. Have another big fight over who goes first. Kid who cries the loudest wins. Adult stupid enough to play goes last.
4. Draw card from the top of the pile.
5. If you are a kid and don't like what you drew, put the card back and keep drawing until you get the one you want. If you are an adult, move five steps backwards.

I think you get the point.

After years of playing with kids, I've finally figured out why they treat us adults this way: THEY DON'T THINK WE'RE ACTU-

ALLY HUMAN BEINGS. We are the seatbelt dummies, don't you know, just waiting to be acted upon.

I first realized that kids regard us as the merest props in their games when my oldest son, Philip, was a preschooler heavily into *Star Wars* action figures. One afternoon when there wasn't much doing, he asked if I'd play *Star Wars* with him and I said yes. In a flash he divided his toys into two piles—one for him, one for me.

"Hey," I said, "how come you get Han and Leia and Luke, and I only get these guys with three eyeballs?"

Philip proceeded as though he hadn't heard me. Mainly because he hadn't.

"Okay," he said, "you make a base for your guys underneath the couch."

"But I was thinking I'd like to make my base on top of the coffee table."

Philip gave me a look which plainly said only a moron would build a base on top of a coffee table, so in the end I made it underneath the couch just like he said.

Finally, we were ready to play.

"Line up in attack formation," he said in his Han Solo voice.

"Heh, heh, heh," I said in my best bad guy voice, "We've got a little surprise planned for Captain Solo."

"Duh, Mom," Philip said.

"Duh what," I said.

"That's not how you play."

"Well then how do you play?" I wanted to know.

As it turned out these were the rules I forgot to read:

> 1. Philip (a) does all the voices and (b) decides what happens next.
> 2. Mom occasionally makes one of her guys with the three eyeballs jump up and down in fright. But only if Philip says it's okay.

As a result of countless experiences like this one, I've decided to swear off playing games with kids forever. This is really it. No more *Star Wars*, *Candyland*, or tennis. Hey, deal me out.

My dad, when he hears this, lifts an amused eyebrow because, after all, he always played with us—in the pool, on the front lawn, around the dining room table covered with games like *Chutes and Ladders*. Furthermore, he acted like he was having fun. *Fun*, if you can believe it. Even that time he took me golfing when I was fourteen and my Snottiness Hormones were at their peak. I can still see us—him packing around clubs for the both of us, me following along in sandals and hot pants, flipping layered bangs out of my eyes and whining about how hot it was.

So, Dad, this one's for you with heaps of love and respect.

And gratitude for years of the important games well-played.

The Stare

*E*ven though we are a very enlightened, consciousness-raised gen-eration, I still think that there are some things our own parents did much better than we do when it comes to raising children. I espe-cially felt this way last spring when I took my kids to the zoo.

I decided to take my kids to the zoo because all parents are now required by federal law to give their children the educational experi-ence of watching a lot of large, very stupid-looking animals munch hay and scratch themselves in embarrassing places. So I invited my mother to join us and off we went to the zoo where everybody, I'm sad to report, had a thoroughly miserable time.

The problem, of course, was that my children were interested in all the wrong things, which always makes me grumpy. They were in-terested in the water fountains and the straw dispensers and the ma-chines where you can buy Official Deer Food. They also wanted to flush toilets in the bathrooms and fiddle with garbage can lids. After that they ran around in circles, blasting each other with pretend lasers and accidentally bumping into elderly women who then swatted them with heavy purses.

The only animals my children displayed any interest in at all were a pair of frisky rhinos, which, in turn, were only interested in each other. This frequently happens at zoos in the spring, I am told.

"Look, Mom!" my kids screamed. "What are they doing now?"

"Ha, ha!" I answered nervously. "Now what do you say we go buy some more deer food?"

When we got in the car to go home, they started to whine.

"We want to ride the train. Remember, you said we could and then we didn't. We want to ride the train. Please. Please!"

"Don't whine," I said.

"You and your brothers never used to whine," my mother piped up.

"Of course we whined," I said. "All kids whine."

"You didn't," she said, and then she added, "because I didn't al-low it."

I thought about this for a minute and decided she could be right after all. I didn't do a lot of things my kids routinely do because I didn't want to risk getting *The Stare*. This was a patented look my mother gave her offspring that said, "If you continue to behave in that thoroughly obnoxious manner, you will go to your bedroom and stay there until you are so old that all your teeth have fallen straight out of your head."

I remember one memorable occasion when my mother gave me *The Stare*. We were eating Sunday dinner which meant that I was busy smacking my lips and leaving milk moustaches all over my mouth.

"Let's not eat like piggies!" Mom reminded me cheerfully.

For some reason I thought this would be a very good opportunity to try out a little joke on her. "Oink! Oink!" I answered.

The room went completely silent. My father, my brothers, the dog eating our shoes under the table—they all looked at me like I'd lost my mind.

"Excuse me?" my mother said politely. Then she gave me *The Stare* which promptly caused me to melt away not unlike the witch with the green face in *The Wizard of Oz* and I was never seen or heard from again. Not only that but I have never said oink oink at the dinner table again.

So when my mother says we never whined, I'm inclined to believe her. My own kids, on the other hand, like to whine and are pretty darn good at it. Just last night, in fact, they were all emitting Olympic-class whines because I checked out the *Excita-Bike* Nintendo game from Sinclair when what they really wanted was *Duck Tales*.

Enough is enough, I said to myself. If *Excita-Bike* is good enough for me, it's good enough for them. That's when I decided to try *The Stare* on them. Unfortunately it did not have the desired effect. Instead of reducing them to nervous little puddles of kidlet, they just thought I'd gotten something in my contacts.

For reasons that we don't entirely understand, none of my friends can do *The Stare* either, although their mothers were all Black Belt starers just like mine. My friends and I feel pretty bad about this and have formed a support group to help us deal with our sense of inadequacy. We meet once a week to share our feelings. Then we eat refreshments and play *Excita-Bike* on the Nintendo.

No doubt our mothers are all wondering where they went wrong.

Say Cowabunga, Dude

I've always had recurring nightmares about one thing or another ever since I was a kid.

When I was in junior high school, for instance, I used to dream that I accidentally went to algebra class naked. I'd be sitting there at my desk, listening to the teacher talk about "x" equaling "y," and suddenly I'd realize I didn't have any clothes on.

"Why don't you have any clothes on?" my friend Gigi sitting next to me would ask.

"I don't know," I'd say, starting to panic. "I must have forgotten to put them on before I left this morning."

Then I'd spend the rest of the dream trying to figure out how I was going to get from algebra class (point x) to my locker (point y) without anybody noticing me. Of course there were variations of this dream. Sometimes I dreamed I went to U.S. History naked, too.

I no longer dream about going to algebra without my clothes on, possibly because I don't take algebra anymore, but I still have recurring nightmares. I dream, for instance, that I'm invited to a party only I realize once I get there that it isn't really a party after all—it's AN OPPORTUNITY TO SELL ME AMWAY—whereupon I faint dead away and everybody spends the rest of my dream trying to revive me with cleaning fluids.

Lately, however, I've been dreaming that I call up my friend Cyndie and offer to take her six children to Olan Mills Portrait Studio to have their picture taken. I pick up the phone and before I can stop them, the words, "Hey, why don't you let me take your kids to Olan Mills this afternoon!" leap straight off my tongue.

Now Cyndie's children are very attractive, very nice children, but I always wake up from one of these dreams in a huge sweat because taking children of any kind to have their pictures done is my idea of hell. You have to comb hair and coordinate outfits so that you look just like the Osmond Brothers, and you have to find socks—socks, for petessake—even though it's a well-known fact that the mates to your family's socks disappeared along with the dinosaurs a very long time ago. Then, on your way over to the studio, the kids find old gum in the car and stick it in their hair.

This was probably why my own parents never had our pictures taken when we were kids. Besides, they were afraid I'd show up without any clothes on. As a result, we were the only family in Provo, Utah, that did not have a family portrait sitting on the piano next to the plastic grapes.

We were mavericks, don't you know.

So because of my upbringing I never did see the point of family portraiture except as a way of documenting all the stupid ways you used to wear your hair.

Not too long ago, however, I got a phone call from someone with an extremely happy voice telling me I could win something if I just answered her question correctly.

"Okay," I said. "Shoot."

"Which of the following three individuals were once president of the United States: Martin Van Buren, Millard Fillmore, Grover Cleveland?"

When I answered after much thought, she did a cheer in my ear and told me I'd won three sittings for the price of one at a local portrait studio.

So I went, and I'm still trying to recover.

For starters, all of my kids resented the fact they had to dress up even though (a) it wasn't Sunday and (b) nobody in the family had died. Furthermore, my four-year-old son Dylan *would not under any circumstances* wear shoes because, as even the village idiot knows, Ninja Turtles don't wear shoes. Not even when they have their Sunday pants on. So I just said to the photographer, please be sure to take the picture of Dylan's head and not of his feet. Also it would help if everybody would just say "Cowabunga" instead of "Cheese."

Talk about your nightmares.

The funny thing, of course, is that the picture actually turned out kind of cute. My four boys—their hair combed and their faces clean—are sitting together in a little group, smiling brightly, and wearing most of their clothes.

Only two of them had their eyes crossed.

How to Tell Children from Adults

When Philip was in kindergarten, he came home from school one day with this interesting bit of information.

"Mom," he said, "do you know what happens when you get bit by a bat?"

He didn't give me a chance to prove that I, too, am up on bats. Before I could shine, he continued, "If you get bit by a bat, you have to go to the hospital where they give you lots of shots and stuff in your stomach. Then you sit around and wait to see if you get rabies."

At this point Philip paused and looked thoughtful. "So, Mom," he said finally, "that's why I don't stick around with bats."

I couldn't help but think this represented a milestone in Philip's psychological development. It showed me that Philip had begun to think in terms of causes and effects.

I have all sorts of little tricks to help me separate the adults from the children in my life. Children, I have found, very rarely carry meter change, two forms of I.D., a Video Shop membership, Huggies coupons, lay-away slips, Visa carbons from Don's Husky, and Triple Cash Bingo cards in their wallets. In fact, children very rarely carry wallets. This in itself is a tell-tale sign of tender age. Adults, on the other hand, hardly ever collect things like Battle Beasts, dinosaur stickers, and Garbage Pail Kids cards. Furthermore, they do not fill used Dixie cups with bits of gravel and glass and put them in their underwear drawer. Also adults never order Happy Meals at McDonald's for themselves.

As useful as these devices are, however, the differences they reveal between grownups and children are superficial, matters of style rather than substance. The true difference between them relates to their ability to see a cause-and-effect relationship. Adults more or less understand that if they jump on Mother's furniture with their shoes on, Mother will breath fire. Children, on the other hand, haven't got a clue and jump away with demented glee.

The truth is that children have very little sense that this follows that or that follows this. So caught up in the moment are they that they cannot look ahead to see what the moment will eventually bring.

I first made this observation long before I had children of my own. I noticed that children have no conception of cause and effect the summer I babysat Sam and Mike.

Sam and Mike were two little boys whom I called the Awful Brothers. The Awful Brothers were especially awful at night when I put them to bed. At that time they became positively wild, turning into night-loving little animals that ripped down curtain rods and left nasty looking marks on each other's arms. To halt the destruction, I tried giving the Awful Brothers very specific instructions when I locked them up at night. "I do not want you to remove screens from the windows or take the closet door off its hinges. Now, if you do any of these things I will call Dan-O and tell him to book you."

In my mind, at least, this summed up my expectations pretty well. So imagine my surprise when the Awful Brothers still kicked holes in their walls. When I then stormed into their bedroom like a one-woman SWAT team, they gave me slightly puzzled expressions that seemed to say, "Now have we met before?"

I used to blame the behavior of the Awful Brothers on their Awful Mother. Now that I have children of my own, however, I'm understandably reluctant to blame a kid entirely on his parent. No, the true problem with the Awful Brothers was that they could not see a connection between their antics and my frantics.

This is certainly true of my own children. Even though I predict for them with startling accuracy what will happen if they stick their tongues on ice cube trees or pull the tail of our sleeping cat, they persist in doing these things. Then when things shake down exactly the way I said they would, my children act surprised and betrayed. They go into their Major League Windups and let loose with a torrent of tears.

All of this just reinforces my belief that the ability to understand causality is acquired—much as a taste for raw fish or important films where the people speak in subtitles. There's nothing natural about seeing how one thing leads to another. So as a parent you just keep plugging away, doing your best, explaining things over and over although no one but the family dog seems to be listening. And then he's only faking it. But then one day a light goes on inside your child's mind and it becomes perfectly clear to him. Yes! he says to himself. It's really true after all! Every single word of it!

If you stick around with bats, you get rabies!

The Information Gap

*E*verybody knows there's an information explosion going on these days. Every time you turn around there's some more information hanging out on a street corner, whistling an airy tune, and filing its fingernails, just waiting for you to notice it.

My kids come home daily with new information about one subject or another. Not too long ago Alec and I had the following conversation.

> **ALEC**: Do you know how they made root beer in the olden days?
> **MOM**: No. I was absent from class the day they had that lecture.
> **ALEC**: They made it out of beer and roots, Mom. For real.

So, in case you've ever wondered about it, that's how they used to get root beer, and you have my permission to pass this along to all your friends and associates absolutely free of charge.

My kids are full of information about plenty of other things, too, including scorpions, which have now taken the place of dinosaurs as their favorite natural history subject.

Actually, I have to take the blame for this since on our way to Phoenix over spring break I did give them my well-known "Social Dynamics of Scorpion Communities" lecture in which I point out that there are basically two kinds of scorpions—Shark scorpions and Jet scorpions. These guys hang around Arizona all day, insulting each other and making pointed remarks about mothers and so forth, until things heat up enough that they decide to have a rumble in an empty schoolyard. But not until they sing a few songs by Leonard Bernstein first.

The only reason I even mentioned all this to my kids is so that they would think twice about falling in with scorpions on our vacation. They, however, assumed that I am very interested in scorpions and have been sharing the following information with me ever since.

1. WHERE THE WORLD'S BIGGEST SCORPION LIVES— at the bottom of Bryce Canyon in Southern Utah.

2. HOW TO KILL A SCORPION—hit it on the top of the head.

3. WHAT SCORPIONS LIKE TO EAT—people.

Also the way you tell boy scorpions from girl scorpions is that boy scorpions never stop to ask directions.

Now this is an example of information my kids have which I do not particularly want. There is information, however, which they don't bother to share with me that I really need. I refer to this phenomenon as the Information Gap.

My latest experience with the Information Gap occurred a few weeks ago. It was a Saturday night, and everybody was in my bedroom. The kids were watching our television, while Ken and I were getting ready to go out. Meanwhile the baby was pulling the telephone off the hook and pretending to talk to George Bush, just like he always does.

There was a knock at the door.

"Can you get that?" I said to Philip.

He didn't budge because he wanted to see what letter Vanna turned over next.

"*Please!*"

Reluctantly, Philip did what I asked. I was busy bathing the baby when he returned to watch *Wheel of Fortune*, and since he didn't say anything, I assumed it had been a neighbor kid at the door.

Which of course was a seriously stupid assumption to make because when I went downstairs myself five minutes later to check on something, there were two uniformed officers standing in the front room waiting for me. I felt just like I was in an episode of *CHIPS*.

"Is everything all right here, ma'am?" Erik Estrada asked.

"I—I don't know," I stammered. "Is it?"

"We received a 911 call from this address," Larry Wilcox responded.

"I don't remember calling," I said, but then who knew? Maybe I was the character with amnesia.

"Do you have any kids that might have been playing around with the telephone?"

"I do have children, but I know for a fact they were watching *Wheel of Fortune*," I answered. "They can't tear themselves away."

Not even long enough to mention that I have a couple of police officers in my house.

Well, the officers finally figured out that the baby—the *baby* for petessake—had put in the call, which is apparently something babies all over the Salt Lake Valley do at least once a day, they told me. I apologized profusely and the officers, who were much kinder to us than we deserved, said goodnight.

As I watched them pull away in their squad car, on their way to bust some more babies, I thought to myself that it certainly would have been nice if Philip had informed me that there were a couple of policemen at our door. When I asked why he hadn't, he looked at me like I'd taken too many scorpion stings in the head and said, "Because, Mom, you didn't ask."

Pretty darn silly of me, don't you agree?

Teenagori

My four younger sons and I were in the car, waiting for the fourteen-year-old who lives at our house to materialize so we could finally leave on our little weekend trip. At last he emerged, laden with the items he needed to insure that his journey was a safe and pleasant one. In one hand he carried a bag of treats from Sinclair not to be confused with anyone else's treats from Sinclair, while in the other he had a stack of CD's not to be confused with anyone else's CD's. Also he was in disguise—baseball cap and sunglasses—so that no one would recognize him and thereby realize he was actually *doing something with his family.*

When he got to the car, he announced that he was the guy riding shotgun and kicked everybody else out of the front seat except for me simply because I'm the one with a license even though he already knows more about driving than I ever will. Then he assumed control over the various sound system knobs in our car and leaned back, settling his brain for a long winter's nap and so forth.

Well, ever since that trip I've been very busy keeping a mental list of all the little signs that say we have a fourteen-year-old boy lurking about the premises. Here's what the list looks like.

1. Every radio in every room is turned on full blast even though he's in the family room watching ESPN.
2. That pack of 500 frozen Lynn Wilson bean and cheese burritos you bought yesterday is already gone.
3. It's twenty below outside, his coat is still hanging in the closet, and he's out there.
4. The phone is never for you any more.
5. He flinches if you accidentally touch the hair it took him twenty minutes to blow-dry.
6. There's a trail of shoes through your house that look like they belong to Big Foot.
7. He fills up a whole couch when he sits down.

8. The only time he notices anybody else in the family is when they do something to irritate him. Like breathe.
9. You never even saw the *Sports Illustrated* swimsuit issue this year.
10. The living room lights flicker whenever he makes a pretend slam-dunk in his bedroom upstairs.
11. There's no hot water left for you to take a shower in the morning.
12. Every radio in every room is turned on full blast even though he's in the family room watching ESPN with a full gaggle of teenage boys who look just like him.

Actually, I'm not really complaining. As teenage-type people go, my oldest son and his friends are very nice ones. About the only time they get on my nerves, in fact, is when they patronize me.

Patronizing adults, unfortunately, is something adolescents do as naturally as turning on a radio, then leaving the room. They think we're all big dorks. We wear dorky clothes and listen to dorky music and hang out with dorky friends and have dorky jobs to pay for those dorky cars we love to drive to dorky destinations such as the beauty shop to get dorky haircuts. We're just too dorky to live, don't you know.

So, as I say, teenagers have no choice but to automatically patronize dorks like us. Take what happened to me the other day. I was in the kitchen throwing an unusually fine fit (my fits overall have improved with age, I'm pleased to report) because the house was such a wreck. Well, my younger kids were responding appropriately—i.e., groveling and promising they'd never leave knives with peanut butter all over the counter again, when the fourteen-year-old walked in and observed my performance. Finally, in a completely calm and thoroughly patronizing voice he said, "Gee, Mom, you're being such a psycho-wench right now."

This pretty much stopped me cold. I've been called a lot of things in my life, but this was the first time anybody had ever thought to call me a psycho-wench.

I confess at first my feelings were hurt. I did a quick review of the Great Psycho-Wenches of History and felt that to be included in their company was hardly flattering. Take Aunt Esmeralda in *Bewitched*, for example. Now there's a psycho-wench for you. As you'll recall, Aunt Esmeralda is Samantha's goofy relative who keeps doing things like accidentally turning Darren's head into a lamp shade and so on. Frankly, she's not somebody I wanted to be when I grew up.

The more I thought about it, however, the more I liked the name. Psycho-Wench. It's kind of snappy, kind of out there, don't you know. Also, people might respect you if you had a nickname like that. They might not give you any (a) lip or (b) sass because who knows what Psycho-Wench will do next. You could even start a club with other mothers of fourteen-year-old boys and call it Psycho-Wenches-R-Us. You could all show up in matching jackets and scare people at soccer games where nobody will ever dare make you feel bad because you forgot the half-time treats again.

Yeah. I'm beginning to think this has definite possibilities.

Goodbye, Donatello

I used to be the mother of a turtle.

Of course we didn't know when he was born that he was a turtle. Unlike Stuart Little's parents who knew immediately that they had a mouse for a son, we assumed with his red face and breath of hair he was simply another splendid boy baby like his brothers before him, so we gave him a good Welsh name in honor of his maternal ancestors.

Dylan.

He answered to it for awhile, too, but when he turned three, we learned that we had been mistaken about who he really was. He shared his true turtle identity with us then, and told us his name was Donatello although we, because he loved us, could call him Don for short.

Don used to wear green pajamas and headbands long after his brothers had put on their jeans and gone to school. Sometimes he wore a huge white shirt over his pajamas, but only if he were taking karate lessons from Splinter that day. Frankly, I never got a very good look at Splinter, although he was a frequent guest in our home. Don assured me, however, that Splinter was right there in front of me, so I tried to be polite even though, to tell you the truth, I felt like I was talking to the air.

Don and Splinter used to go outside on the front lawn when the weather was fine and practice their kicks. I stood at the window and watched. Don liked the flying kicks best. He'd run, his bright hair flapping about his ears, then leap into the air and boot his leg out hard as he could. No doubt Splinter's kicks were high and deadly, too, although I really can't say for sure.

Don specialized in machines. He took an ordinary boy's bed with a Mickey Mouse comforter, for example, and turned it into the Turtle Blimp just like that, a flying machine capable of cruising at unusually high altitudes thereby allowing Don to elude the bad guys who sometimes slipped into our house when no one was watching.

Don could also take ordinary household items and turn them into Turtle-Coms whenever he needed to get in touch with somebody fast. Many was the time I saw Don talking intently into a shoe that he had transformed into a communicator thanks to his mechanical magic.

Occasionally it was a little embarrassing to have a turtle for a son. Don didn't like to leave home without his weapon, which meant we went everywhere—the neighbor's, the store, the library—with a plastic baseball bat, i.e. "bow," stuffed down the back of his shirt. Once Don even took his weapon to church, although I didn't realize it until an older woman in the congregation nervously pointed it out to me. Frankly, I don't know why she was so surprised. After all our family did accidentally take a dog to church once which seems a lot weirder to me than taking a baseball bat, although I'm sure something like that depends on your perspective.

I've been thinking about Don quite a bit because of a memory I had this morning when I stepped onto the porch and felt a flash of fall. We had a dog when I was a kid, an elkhound, who used to perk to life again when the cool weather set in. She'd run outside first thing each morning to sniff the air, her bushy tail looped over her back like a question mark. The colder it got, the more she quivered with excitement. When the snow finally flew, that dog went completely crazy. She'd charge outside where she'd leap and roll and throw snow with her snout.

For years I observed her giddy routine and didn't think much about it except to laugh as I left for school. Now that she's gone, however, along with that part of my life, I find the memory of it both sad and sweet and full of unexpected force.

Don left us so gradually that I hardly noticed until the day I saw a leggy six-year-old with a gap-toothed grin sitting at Don's place across from me at the dinner table. His name is Dylan, and he likes baseball.

My life is an accumulation of small events, most of them supremely ordinary—chopping onions for dinner, saying hello to the mailman, combing a child's hair, stooping over to pick up the morning paper, dialing the number of a neighbor, half-listening to my wind chimes, sharpening pencils, gossiping at work, over-eating on Sunday, feeding a cat, pulling a weed, picking up clothes, watching the news at ten, stepping onto my porch first thing in the morning when the air is still new and full of birds. I wonder which of all these events will come back to me as memory, like that of my dog lost in silliness or of Don leaping straight into the air?

And which of them, I wonder, like the brief sight of violets in the spring, will take my heart in the passing?

Fashion Folly

Fashion Folly

I'll never forget the day I took our three oldest boys to the doctor's office for penicillin shots. As they pulled down their sweat pants one by one, I realized that nobody was wearing any underwear. Sometime between last night's baths and the present moment, they'd all ditched the He-Man underoos and now they were standing before me, the pediatrician, and his nurse, advertising the fact.

It was one of those lows in my mothering career. A real nadir, don't you know.

"Just for the record," I said with as much dignity as possible, "I, at least, have my underwear on."

"SO IS THIS A GUY THING OR WHAT?" I asked the three of them on the way home. Then I proceeded to give them the kind of lecture that I imagine June never had to give the Beav—i.e., that some things in life, such as wearing underwear to the doctor's office, are not options.

I called Ken as soon as I got home and wailed with embarrassment.

"What did you expect?" he said philosophically when I was finished. "They are your children after all."

"Excuse me?" I responded with what the French call *hauteur*. "I never leave home without my underwear."

"Of course you don't," he soothed. "It's just that you're always the first to admit that you have a certain flair for underdressing."

He had a point there. Take what happened to me last weekend when my mother invited me to attend a luncheon and fashion show with her. I left home wearing a sporty double-knit pantsuit that was (mostly) clean. Also I combed my hair.

I should have known I was in serious trouble when my mother met me out front looking like she was in the middle of doing a fashion shoot for *Vogue*. Things got worse when we went inside. Everyone present was doing (a) linen, (b) silk, and (c) mousse. Also they were all heavily into large Joan Collins-type accessories.

Needless to say, I did *not* see myself coming and going. "How did you know what to wear?" I hissed in my mother's ear.

She shrugged helplessly the way she used to when I was in the fifth grade and somebody told her I'd been throwing spitwads on the school bus again. "Well, it is a luncheon after all, Sweetheart."

I gave one of those bitter snorts you're always reading about. "I'll tell you what I think. It's a conspiracy. Everybody here received an invitation that said, 'Please RSVP and also really dress up so that Ann Cannon will feel like she did the day she got married.'"

My wedding was, perhaps, my most notable fashion disaster. All of my bridesmaids and most of the people who came, including the adolescent girls who served the nut cups, were better dressed than I was.

The idea of wearing my mother's wedding dress seemed like a good one at first. It was, after all, a splendid satin number with a very serious train. That it clearly looked better on my mother than it did on me didn't matter much. The sentiment of the thing was what counted. Besides, I would wear flowers in my hair and people would say I was ravishing.

"You want to wear a wreath on your head?" my mother asked when I told her of my plans. It was obvious she thought I'd been sitting in the sun too long. Or maybe she thought I was ovulating.

"A garland, not a wreath," I told her. "Lots of people do." This was, after all, the 1970s.

"You want to wear a wreath instead of a veil or a nice little hat with a bit of net over your face?"

I held firm, and in the end she called the florist who said he would deliver the garland the afternoon of the event. Such was my faith in his ability that I never even bothered to look at it until thirty minutes before my reception.

I was in the reception center restroom with one of my bridesmaids when I opened the florist's box and saw my garland for the first time. Instead of a romantic confection of baby's breath, rosebuds, and daisies, it was made up of evergreens, not unlike the shrubs growing in front of my parents' home.

I gaped.

"Maybe it looks better on," my friend said doubtfully.

With trembling hands, I reached for the garland and placed it squarely on my head.

"Oh dear," sighed my friend. "You look just like the Ghost of Christmas Present."

So that was that, and in the end I attended my reception absolutely and completely bare-headed.

Underdressed, as usual.

Fashion Folly II: The Pool Party

*I*f your children were invited to a "pool party," how would you dress them?

    A. In a swimming suit
    B. In a swimming suit
    C. In a swimming suit
    D. In a swimming suit

Admittedly, my experience with pool parties has been somewhat limited. I didn't exactly grow up in the kind of neighborhood where people regularly threw parties of the pool variety. In fact, the closest I ever got to going to one was when I'd meet a few friends for the Free Swim at ye olde municipal pool where we mostly took hot showers and tried to figure out ways to get Sugar Babies out of the vending machine without spending any money.

Still, a pool party is a pool party, right? You show up in a suit you hope makes you look just like that model in the catalogue, then you lounge around the deck sampling a few Doritos along with the guacamole and bean dip. With any luck, you don't even have to get wet before going home. Nothing to it.

Wrong.

Last summer our family of seven moved for a year to a toney neighborhood in New York where we more or less arrived like the Joads in *The Grapes of Wrath*. Still, people have been very kind to us, inviting us to gatherings and so forth just like the Victorians used to have the Elephant Man over for the odd cup of tea.

One of the first soirees to which we were invited was a children's pool party.

"Hey, kids," I said. "You're going to a pool party. Just think what fun you'll have doing jackknives and so forth off the diving board. By the time the party's through, everybody will know who the Cannon boys are!"

When it was time to go, I told my kids to put on their suits. And then because we're in such a swanky place, I told them to (a) comb their hair and (b) put on T-shirts, all of which I thought was very far-sighted of me. My kids would be both classy and appropriate.

Especially appropriate, don't you know.

Some of you may have guessed by now that I have an unfortunate tendency to get the dress thing all wrong, so being appropriate is very important to me. Usually, I am underdressed for any given occasion, although I have been known to show up like a geek in a skirt when everybody else is wearing jeans.

It's like everybody but me went to gym class for a special matura-tion program about what clothes you should wear for which occasion.

I don't come by this lack of wardrobe sense naturally. The woman who gave me life has never once made a fashion misstep. Even if she's the only woman in a room wearing a pair of slacks, she looks so totally dynamite that everyone else assumes they're all wearing the wrong thing.

"How do you do that?" I ask her.

She shrugs helplessly, because the last thing she would ever want to do is make somebody feel uncomfortable.

"I know," I say, giving her a bitter snort. "It's because you were a rodeo queen when you were nineteen years old, isn't it. Once you've worn a tiara on your brim, you have an aura of confidence that never deserts you."

I, on the other hand, was not a rodeo queen, which may explain my whole fashion problem. Still, I try very hard to get it right. And I tried the night of the pool party.

This is what happened.

We went to the pool at the appointed hour where we were greeted by a bevy of children, none of whom was wearing a swimming suit. In-stead, this is what they had on:

A. The girls were wearing Laura Ashley-type dresses.
B. The boys were wearing khaki slacks and blue blazers.
C. I am telling you the truth.

So there we were at a pool party wearing, of all the stupid things, SWIMMING SUITS! Even my kids picked up on the fact that they were the only people present not wearing shoes.

So we sat around the pool with everyone else for an hour or so, eating the kind of hot dogs Martha Stewart would make if Martha Stewart made hot dogs and trying our best to blend.

On the way home Ken turned to me and said, "Well, you got one thing right—everybody now knows who the Cannon boys are."

"This isn't fair!" I stuck my head out the car window and wailed at the cosmos not unlike Job in the Old Testament. "How was I supposed to know how people in New York dress their children for pool parties?"

In the end Providence smiled on me. When I went shopping the very next day, I happened to wander by the Brooks Brothers outlet and noticed that they were closing out all their boy's navy blue blazers. I marched right in and bought one for each of my boys.

So now when it's May and the swimming season is almost upon us, I'll be ready.

"You're invited to another pool party?" I'll say to my children.

"No problemo! Your jackets, my sons, are hanging in the closet."

Jazz Dancer

So there I was, listening to the car radio while hauling my four-year-old off to preschool.

"Meet your favorite Utah Jazz Dancer after tonight's game!" said the announcer. "Talk to her! Get her autograph! Don't miss out on this fabulous, once-in-a-lifetime experience!"

That's all I needed to hear, and before I knew it, I was very busy imagining Jazz Dancers after the game, all smiles and hair, ready to meet their adoring public.

But what if there was one Jazz Dancer nobody wanted to meet? What if all the Jazz Dancers had huge lines waiting to get their autographs except for one? And what if she just stood there in her snappy little lycra outfit, smiling as hopefully as a seventh-grade girl at a junior high dance, and still nobody came? Before long people would start to feel sorry for her. They would avoid making eye contact and she would have to wonder what was wrong with her until finally some very sweet older woman asked for her autograph out of pure kindness.

The more I thought about all this, the worse I felt. I could feel this Jazz Dancer's pain as though it were my own, mostly because I knew in my heart of hearts that if I were a Jazz Dancer, the same terrible thing would happen to me. No doubt about it, I would be the one that everybody ignored.

I tried to imagine why people would ignore *moi* that night after the game. Maybe I got confused and put my clothes on the wrong way. I did that once. I was standing in front of my freshman English class, mentioning a little something about (a) subjects and (b) verbs, when I realized *my skirt was on backwards*. I let out a brief, terse scream which I did not explain to my startled students who later walked away from class that day more convinced than ever that only The Truly Insane major in English.

There could be other reasons people were ignoring me, as well. Maybe there was a problem with my hair. Bad perm, perhaps? Bad cut? Bad color? Of course I've tried them all. My hair and what it's not doing right, in fact, is a source of endless concern to me and my mother. We've even been seriously considering buying one of those Hair Genies you see advertised on television at 1:00 in the morning. It seems like a pretty amazing invention, allowing you to put your hair in an air bun with one hand while driving your car with another. I think it holds real possibilities for me. Next thing you know I'll be starring in an all-new infomercial, wearing my Jazz Dancer outfit and explaining how the Hair Genie changed my life.

But I digress.

At any rate I was in a rare snit about the whole Jazz Dancer thing by dinnertime. How dare people not stand in my line! How dare they ignore me, thereby making me the object of pity among my Jazz Dancer sisters with their lines all the way out to West Valley City. To paraphrase your Shakespeare, do I not bleed when people prick me? Do I not laugh when they tickle me, and die when they poison me? Am I not a human being and so forth, too?

Even my kids sitting around the table noticed something was bothering me.

"Like, what's the matter with you?" my fourteen-year-old asked. Mostly he was irritated that I was in a bad mood since being in a bad mood is supposed to be his job now that he's in junior high school.

"Where were you guys when I needed somebody to stand in my line?" I retorted.

The words *speechless* and possibly even *dumbstruck* pretty much sum up my family's response at that precise moment.

"Do you think," Ken ventured gently, "that winter is getting to you?"

I paused. Perhaps he had a point. After all, when the days are short and dark and cold, one can be seized by wild and unpleasant imaginings.

"Just a few more weeks, Ann," he soothed, "and then it will be spring."

Already the crocuses and pansies, the violets and daffodils are stirring. The days are lengthening. The breezes are warming. I can step out on my front porch and taste the change of seasons in the air.

Spring!

Soon my boys will start their endless games of baseball on the front lawn. Soon the tree outside my window will be filled with bird noise again. Soon the air will hang thick with the scent of lilacs, re-minding me of all the lilacs from springs before.

Ken's right. It's almost here.

Time to hang up the old Jazz Dancer uniform for good.

Hair Anxiety

I think hair is one of the world's stupidest inventions.

So what if it keeps your head warm in the winter. BIG DEAL. That hardly compensates for the fact that hair is nothing but a nuisance the rest of the time. The very worst thing about hair, of course, is that you have to decide what to do with it. Sometimes I think my whole life has been spent in pursuit of the Perfect Hairdo.

I get this obsession about hair from my mother who truly believes that if you can just find the right hairdo, all of the problems in your life will be solved automatically. Whenever I used to talk to my mother about the problems of being a teenager, she'd fix me with a sympathetic stare, then say, "Do you think we ought to perm your hair, Sweetheart?" If I'd recently had a perm, she'd try another tact and ask me if I wanted to do something to the color instead. Usually I said yes—maybe my problems really would go away if I looked like a totally different person the next day—and so Mom and I would get two Tabs from the fridge, crawl in her Volkswagen bug, drive to the nearest Skagg's Drugstore, and check out the hair color products.

"What do you think," she'd say as we surveyed the rows of Miss Clairol together. "Do you want to be a Winter Wheat this time?"

During one giddy summer my mother and I dyed my hair four times. I went from being a blonde to a brunette to a redhead back to a brunette. And we frosted it after that. My family refers to that period as The Summer Ann Had an Identity Crisis. It's not that I didn't know who I was so much. It's just that I kept forgetting what I looked like. Whenever I'd see myself in the mirror first thing each morning, I'd jump in surprise, then say, "Oh that's right—I have red hair now."

When I asked a friend why people (including my Grandpa who always calls me Rhonda) never recognize me from one time to the next, he said, "I think it's because you fool around a lot with your hair." It's true. I do fool with my hair. Although I haven't dyed my hair since I got married and moved out of my mother's house, I still try on different hairstyles in much the same way I imagine that Queen Elizabeth tries on hats—and mostly with the same disastrous results. One ultra-cropped haircut I had awhile ago looked positively institutional. Another had bangs so short that I looked a little like Mamie Eisenhower at the Inaugural Ball. For awhile I even had buffalo hair just like all those girls on my then-favorite soap, *Days of Our Lives*.

Telling my hairdresser who I wanted to look like, in fact, used to be my favorite technique for describing the hairdo I wanted. I'd say, "Why don't you give me buffalo hair, just like all those girls on *Days of Our Lives?*" and sure enough I'd walk away from the salon with the best darned buffalo hair you ever saw. I abandoned this technique, however, after I once told a stylist to make me look like Jacqueline Bisset. He sniffed and said, "Well, I'll see what I can do from the neck up—"

I do take some comfort from the fact that I am not the only woman who worries about her hair. Most of the women I know worry about their hair. In fact, so many women worry about their hair these days that the American Psychological Association (APA) has recently recognized a disorder known as Hair Anxiety. Here are the three main symptoms of Hair Anxiety, which I believe is one of the major problems facing Americans today.

1. Every day you wonder what you ought to do to your hair.
2. Every day you ask your husband what you ought to do to your hair.
3. Every day your husband tells you he doesn't care what you do to your hair so please, please don't ask again.

For awhile there it looked like none of my own children would ever have to experience Hair Anxiety because I only have boys. I learned how wrong I was when I took Dylan, who was three years old, to the barber shop. The shop was staffed by two jolly barbers with round faces who looked like they might well enjoy singing snatches of Austrian folk songs as they worked. They smiled at Dylan and invited him to sit in a chair which Dylan reluctantly did. Dylan managed to sit patiently as they wrapped the towel around his neck, then draped the plastic smock over his clothes. But when Dylan caught sight of the scissors, it was all over. He began to scream. Worse, he began to fidget. Those barbers looked at each other, and then they began rubbing their hands together.

"I think we need—THE STRAP!" cried the head barber.

"Yes, Master," cried his assistant. "The strap! The strap!" "Igor, get me the strap!" cried the head barber.

So Igor, like the good assistant barber he was, dragged his knuckles across the floor to the closet and produced the strap, whereupon they tied Dylan in his seat and proceeded to give him their version of the haircut from hell. It was awful. Dylan cried. I cried. Even my mom cried when I told her about it. Fortunately we both knew exactly what to do to feel better.

We hurried right out and got ourselves a perm.

'Tis the Season for Football

*B*asically, I define football as a game where a group of very large men wearing tights run around trying to hurt each other. I mean it. These guys really do want to rip each other apart because they're ticked off at having to wear such silly outfits. Here they've spent all this time developing manly muscles and the next thing you know some coach is making them wear sissy ballerina pants in front of 60,000 people.

I'd be mad, too.

Then again I don't think wearing tights in public is nearly as bad as wearing boxers, which is what basketball players do. They put on their underwear and off they go to the nearest gym to play a game of pickup with other guys also wearing underwear. So on the basis of clothes alone, I would definitely choose football as my favorite sport.

Actually, I've been going to football games for years. When we were in sixth grade, my friend Gigi and I used to pay a quarter for seats in the end zone where we hooked up with sixth grade boys who engaged in the well-known mating ritual of throwing popcorn at our heads.

We also enjoyed trying out original cheers such as the following:

SAY IT CLEAR!
SAY IT LOUD!
OUR FEET SMELL
AND WE'RE PROUD!

Or something along those lines.

Later, when we were teenagers, Gigi and I went to games mainly to critique uniforms. This was a highly educational experience which basically taught us that you are in very big trouble fashion-wise if, like the University of Wyoming, your school colors happen to be brown and gold because recent scientific evidence strongly suggests that people are ten times more likely to mistake your cheerleaders for a convention of Taco Time employees.

And since we're on the subject of fashion, I really wish the football coaches in this country would make a conscientious effort to stop wearing polyester pants and opt instead for natural fibers such as cotton, linen, or, on special occasions such as bowl games, raw silk.

(By the way, have you noticed how many college players are wearing black shoes again? In my opinion this is a *serious* fashion mistake. White socks and black shoes break the line of the leg.)

Well, as you can imagine, all those years of watching football has given me a thorough grasp of the intricacies of the game—a fact which impresses my friends who are confused by the sport. It's not that hard, I tell them. Basically, what you have are two teams each with eleven players. One team is the offense, the other is the defense. They line up on the field, the center snaps the ball to the quarterback, and then blah, blah, blah, so on and so forth, etcetera, etcetera, until somebody wins the game and we all go home.

See? There's nothing to it.

The only reason why people get confused is that they've been listening to sports announcers too long. Basically, sports announcers are individuals who get paid huge sums of money to be on TV wearing earphones and sitting in lazy-boy recliners while gassing with each other about whatever game they happen to be watching. These people are not always easy to understand. When they cover golf matches, for instance, they sit there and whisper to each other which I personally believe is very rude. I want to stand up like my old third grade teacher, Mrs. Rigby, and say, "Excuse me. Would you mind sharing that with the rest of the class, please?"

When it comes to football, sports announcers stop speaking English altogether. They have conversations like the following:

"This defensive line always does a lot of stunting. What do you think, Bob?"

"I thoroughly agree with your comments about stunting, Bill, and by the way, I like your new suit."

So my advice to you is to forget the sports announcers altogether and concentrate on the game itself. Cheer. Scream. Eat lots of popcorn. Have fun.

And may the team with the best-looking guys win.

Power Whining in the 1990s

When it comes to communicating their desires, kids are much more effective than adults. I came to this conclusion last night after Ken and I had the following discussion for a couple of hours.

> **KEN**: What movie do you want to see tonight?
> **ME**: I don't care. What movie do you want to see?
> **KEN**: I don't care. Whatever movie you want to see—

(CUT TO THE DISTANT FUTURE. ANN AND KEN, COVERED WITH COBWEBS, ARE STILL SITTING AT THE DINING ROOM TABLE, HAVING THIS EXTREMELY BORING CONVERSATION.)

Actually, Ken and I frequently have trouble making decisions about things like movies and restaurants. We're such considerate people, don't you know, that we desire the other person's happiness above all. Also, if the movie is a bust, we feel entitled to blame the spouse who made the decision and MAKE HIS LIFE A LIVING HELL UNTIL THE END OF TIME!

Our kids, on the other hand, are never shy about what they want. They tell us fifty times a day, and then, in case we forget, they fax us memos during recess.

Other parents tell me their children do this, too.

Unfortunately, most kids get what they want more often than they probably should because they employ a very effective technique—i.e., whining.

(WHINING—a force of nature, not unlike tidal waves, which mere mortals such as parents are ultimately powerless to resist.)

Like most children, my kids are not above whining to get what they want. When Dylan was two, for example, he went through a stage where he wanted to take extremely weird stuff like videocassettes and cereal boxes to bed with him. When I told him no, it simply isn't *done,* Dylan let loose with a few hurricane-force whines and I finally relented. Of course, I forgot to mention all this to my mother, who was very confused one night after tucking Dylan in bed.

"Ann," she said emerging from the bedroom, "Dylan is sleeping with his snow boots tonight. He isn't wearing them. They're just there on the pillow next to his head."

I didn't say anything.

Mom fixed me with a stare. "He told me *you* said he could. Is that true?"

Miserable, I nodded.

She didn't say anything, but I could tell she didn't approve. That's when I went mad. I clapped my hands over my ears, just like Quasimodo in *The Hunchback of Notre Dame*, and started to mumble, "I WAS HELPLESS I TELL YOU! HELPLESS!" At that point I ran out of the house and through the streets of Salt Lake City, shrieking. People who saw me shook their heads sadly and said, "Now there goes a noble ruin of a woman."

So, as you can readily see, whining is a very powerful form of communication that gets you *everything* you ever wanted, which is why I have developed the following new theory:

ONLY ADULTS SHOULD BE ALLOWED TO WHINE.

The way I see it, kids nowadays have a lot of adult privileges. For instance, all of them get to stay up and watch the *Tonight Show*, whereas our own mothers made us go to bed by 5:30 in the afternoon, even during Daylight Savings Time. That's why I truly believe we grown-ups should band together and take over one of their privileges, specifically whining.

Besides, we have more to whine about anyway.

Take buying a new swimming suit, for instance. Now there's an experience I can whine about all day long. First of all, there is the utter shame of having to ask the well-moussed sales girl who is definitely (a) younger and (b) more nubile than you for permission to try on a suit. Of course, she's always polite to your face, but you know as soon as she shows you to the dressing room, she tells the other sales girls (who also have advanced degrees in Mousse Engineering) to get a load of the dumpy old broad in 3C.

"Can you believe those legs?" they all squeal. "How does she even dare walk in public on those things?"

And the fluorescent/neon/strobe lights in the dressing rooms!

Dressing room lights have been scientifically proven to make any woman in a bathing suit look fifty years older and fifty pounds heavier, especially if said bathing suit is cut up to a woman's nose. Which all of them are.

"Whatever happened to the swimsuits our mothers used to wear—the ones cut to your knees with tin bras?" I asked a friend of mine. "They weren't pretty, but at least everything you own, whether you want it or not, isn't on display in a suit like that."

She shook her head sadly and said, "I don't know. Let's whine about it, shall we?"

So we did. "Oh, we want a suit, just like the suit that was worn by dear old Mom. *Can we, huh, can we, can we huh? Please? Please oh please oh please—*"

You watch. Any moment now and the swimming suit will be ours!

Reflections on the Fondue

Not long ago when I was pawing through my kitchen cupboard looking for something, I came across an item I hadn't seen for quite a few years—i.e., my old avocado green fondue pot. Naturally, seeing my fondue pot stirred up quite a few memories of Dating in the 1970s since fondue pots, along with eight-track tapes, were certainly an essential prop in the high school courtship rituals of that period.

Basically this is what a date was like back then. You and your friend Gigi would decide to take a couple of boys with prominent sideburns who were in your math class to a girl's choice dance, which naturally meant you both needed to get (a) a new dress with a wide white collar just like the ones Susan St. James used to wear in *MacMillan and Wife*, as well as (b) a new pair of platform shoes.

("*Platform shoes? Platform shoes?*" *our mothers always used to groan.* "*But they're so unattractive. Don't you know what Carol Lawrence always says? Shoes should be slim and unobtrusive so that they don't break the long line of a beautiful leg.*"

Naturally, we rolled our eyes straight back in our heads when our mothers said highly goofy stuff like this. Please. We were sixteen. Why would we want to look like Robert Goulet's ex-wife?)

At any rate, on the night of the dance you got ready by taking a shower and washing your long, straight Susan St. James-type hair with Flex Balsam shampoo after which you covered yourself with a thick cloud of strong perfume such as Youth Dew by Estee Lauder. By the time you walked out the front door with your date, who himself was awash in a sea of Elsha, people downwind could smell the two of you for miles.

Once you were at the dance, you and your date did a combination of the following three things: (1) sat around on the folding chairs against the wall and made nervous small talk, (2) danced, except during the drum solos, and (3) secretly worried about whether or not you might fall off your platform shoes and break your ankle.

Now here's the part where the fondue pot comes in. After the dance you and your date and your friend Gigi and her date met at your house for a nice late-night, candlelit dinner consisting of Caesar salad, warm orange rolls from the Provo Bakery, and raw beef which the four of you then proceeded to stab with little forks and slowly fry—piece by piece—in boiling peanut oil. You had to wait for about twenty minutes between bites. Meanwhile your stomachs were growling just like a pride of hungry lions on the make for a couple of unsuspecting Christians wandering through the woods at night.

Wow. What a gastronomical concept.

Anyway, I started thinking about fondue pots all over again when I was visiting New York City this past week. Not that I ate at any fondue pot restaurants while I was there. Far from it, in fact. On this particular trip I ate at one of your famous four-star chi-chi establishments where you were required to (a) pull your hair back, (b) suck in your cheeks, (c) wear lots of black, and (d) look slightly bored. Naturally I tried my best to fit in. I glanced over the menu, acting like I and my hollow cheekbones didn't care that we couldn't see prices printed anymore. Then, in a world-weary voice that suggested I'd seen the inside of one too many four-star restaurants in my day, I ordered monkfish. I ordered monkfish for the following two reasons: (1) I'd never tasted it before and (2) I'd always wanted to meet a celibate fish. Anyway, I waited around for awhile, looking jaded and so forth, until my meal was served.

This is what it looked like—a little slice of meat resting on a moist bed of greens, most of which I couldn't identify. That was it. No potato or rice. Just a little monkfish, crisply and cleanly presented for my dining pleasure.

I know that I was supposed to go wild about this and start spouting off *eh biens* all over the place. I know my palette was supposed to have spasms of longing at the very sight of that exquisitely prepared monkfish floating serenely in the middle of a large white plate. But suddenly I felt like I was in high school again, crouching furtively around a fondue pot with my little bits of uncooked beef, wondering glumly if my adolescent hunger would ever be satisfied.

It's at times like these that my essential white-trashiness starts to show, not unlike your basic bra strap at a Wednesday night Bingo game. Here's the thing—when it comes right down to it, I want quantity, thank you very much, especially if I'm paying lots of money. This is what happens to people like me who spent their childhood eating

Sunday dinner at Sizzler because one of their dad's buddies was the manager. They want heaps of food on their plates—lots of steak and potato and hefty hunks of cheese toast on the side. They want their salads laced with mayo. They want pie and ice cream for dessert.

Okay, so now my secret's out.

You've probably even guessed that I use Campbell soup whenever I make Cream of Monkfish casserole.

Some Shallow Thoughts on Man's
Best Friend

The True Reason Why Dog Is My Best Friend

*W*hen I took my dog Bogie to a soccer game last Saturday, I couldn't help but notice the general public's reaction to him, which was that they (a) held their noses and (b) fled.

"Weren't you embarrassed?" Ken asked when I told him about the experience later.

"Actually, no," I replied. "It just reinforced my reasons for owning dogs in the first place. No matter how bad I may smell, I know one of the dogs will always smell worse."

They make me look good in comparison, don't you know.

This is particularly true when it comes to intelligence. I'm always amazed by people who talk about how smart their dog is, then cite the fact that the animal can leap five feet into the air and snag a frisbee as evidence. I'm very sorry, but I personally do not believe that (a) jumping and (b) catching frisbees with your teeth are necessarily signs of high intelligence. Hey, you can bet if I hung around in a park all day trying to catch frisbees in my mouth that nobody would call me smart.

The truth is that on the International Stupid Scale, dogs rate a solid ten.

Now before any animal lovers take offense, I need to make it perfectly clear that I respect and admire dogs very much. Often I do nothing but respect and admire dogs all day long. Also some of my best friends are dogs. Over the years I've owned a wide assortment of poodles, boxers, spaniels, terriers, hounds, and mutts, and while I have always found them to be exceptionally charming dinner companions—particularly since they like everything I cook unlike certain other people in my family—I can't honestly say I think they're bright.

Of course they are brighter than quail who have recently bumped cows from first place on the official Dumb Animals of the Earth list. Whenever I drive through the kind of neighborhood where quail hang out, I see them huddled on the side of the road waiting for cars.

"OH NO," they scream and clutch one another in terror when

one finally appears, "LET'S MAKE A RUN FOR THE OTHER SIDE OF THE ROAD WHERE WE'LL BE SAFE!"

Then they run like crazy across the street (while you slam on your brakes) and wait for the next car to show up.

So you see that dogs are definitely smarter than quails.

Still, that isn't saying much. Bogie, for instance, once tried to eat a light bulb. This is the same dog who hasn't figured out that birds actually fly in the air. He just watches their shadows track across the snow, then dives headfirst into the ground every now and then whenever he thinks he can get one.

And then there's Basil. Basil is a very beautiful, very dense English Cocker whom I never take anywhere in the car except to the groomers, which he hates with all his little doggy heart. But does this stop him from wanting to get in the car with me every time I go some place? No. Whenever I open the front door, he bolts out and runs straight to the Jeep because somebody has told him that he and I are going on a date to the prom.

Of course, he practically dies from joy when I actually let him leap into the back seat because it's time to take him to the groomer's again. As I drive down South Temple, I can see him in the rear view mirror, panting happily and yelling "Què pasa, Babe?" at girl dogs out the window.

About half way there, however, I see the light go on in his little brown eyes.

"Whoa, wait a minute here," he thinks. "This is starting to look—what's the word I want? Familiar. Yes, that's it. Familiar. This is starting to look familiar. Could it be that she's taking me to have my hair done?"

"Yes, Basil, it's true," I say to him, "I'm taking you to the groomer's to have your hair done."

"THE GROOMER'S! Oh please, anywhere but THE GROOMER'S! I'm doomed!"

"You're being overly dramatic," I point out.

"I am not! She makes me take a bath and then she puts—what's the word I want? Bows. Yes, that's right. Bows. She puts sissy bows on my ears, and all the other dogs laugh and make mock!"

At this point he sticks his nose under the seat in an effort to hide, but it's no use because I, with my superior intelligence, spot him every single time.

This is just fine with me. Let other people brag about how intelligent their dogs are. I personally wouldn't want a dog I couldn't trick into thinking we were going on a date. Hey, I already have a houseful of kids who think they're smarter than I am.

What on earth would I do with a dog who thinks the same thing?

My Telephone Call with a Social Worker

*D*on't ask me why, but whenever I pick up a telephone, my kids act like I've just given them a big time cue to go berserk. They stand right in front of me while my hand and ear are all tied up, then they start screaming and fighting because they're annoyed at the way the other brother breathes.

Totally charming, I think you'll agree.

This kind of behavior is always distracting, to say the least, but occasionally it's even embarrassing—like the time I called the social worker.

We came home one evening to discover an invitation for a birthday party waiting politely for us on the doorstep. It was for our son Alec from one of his third-grade classmates, and it requested that we R.S.V.P.

I will confess that at times I have been careless about doing this sort of thing, which I have since learned is a major social blunder. I can only attribute my lack of grace in this respect to the fact that I grew up in a very communal town where wedding notices in the local paper routinely said, "The public is invited to attend." It never occurred to us to put "R.S.V.P" on the bottom of anything because none of us could read French anyway. I had to move to Salt Lake City before I realized that civilized people actually like to get a head count before an event so that there's enough food and drink, and so forth.

Anyway, after screwing up on the R.S.V.P. thing a couple of times, I made a resolution some time ago to call my hostess ahead of time to inform her of my plans. That's why I promptly marched inside, birthday party invitation in hand, and called the classmate's mother, a person I don't know extremely well but about whom I've always heard the nicest things. Intelligent, kind, competent are the adjectives people routinely use when describing her. She also happens to be a committed social worker.

So there I was on the phone, having a nice chat with a social worker, when Ken walked into the room where I was and noticed that our dog Irene was nosing through the garbage can, looking for disgusting things to eat.

Dogs eating garbage is one of Ken's big buttons, so he started yelling "IRENE! IRENE! IRENE!" as he reached down to yank her out of the garbage can.

At this precise moment, our oldest son, Philip—who has a heightened sense of the dramatic anyway—walked into the room, assessed the situation, and began yelling, "PLEASE DON'T CHOKE HER, DADDY!"

I just kept on talking like nothing at all was happening at our house, while secretly wondering why we always give our dogs people names instead of dog names. If Ken were to yell "SMUDGIE! SMUDGIE! SMUDGIE!" at the top of his lungs, for instance, no one would assume he was talking to a human being. Yelling "IRENE! IRENE! IRENE!," however, makes him sound like he's going after an elderly aunt with one of her own hat pins, especially when our oldest son is standing there screaming, "PLEASE DON'T CHOKE HER, DADDY!"

Actually, now that I think about it, I realize I come by giving dogs people names naturally. My mom's poodle had the exact same name as my best friend, so whenever my mom yelled at the dog to get off the chair, my friend invariably went flying out of her seat.

But I digress.

I finished up my telephone call as bravely as I could, put down the receiver, then attempted to give everyone—dog included—my version of THE STARE.

"Excuse me, Philip," I said, "but when was the last time you actually saw your father choke a dog?"

He hemmed and hawed, then admitted that to the best of his knowledge he'd never seen his father choke a dog.

"When was the last time you saw your father do *anything* to a dog besides feed it?"

Again Philip had to admit he hadn't seen his father do anything to a dog besides feed it.

Then I turned my attention to Ken. "Didn't you notice I was trying to do the R.S.V.P. thing over the telephone?"

Sheepishly, Ken confessed he hadn't.

Finally, I looked at the dog, Irene. "And you. Why were you eating garbage in the first place?"

She wagged her tail because she thought I was giving her quality time, then she trotted off to eat some more garbage.

As a result of my little experience, I have devised a set of rules one should follow religiously when talking with social workers on the telephone:

1. Do not call a social worker while your dog is eating the garbage.
2. If you must call a social worker while your dog is eating the garbage, use a pay phone.

In the spirit of public service, I pass these rules along absolutely free of charge!

How to Enhance Your Own Self-Esteem

I don't know about others, but I personally believe that being a parent during the Middle Ages was a whole lot easier than it is today. I cite the following reasons:

1. You only had to bathe your kids once a year.
2. You didn't have to nag them about brushing and flossing, mainly because nobody had teeth.
3. They got married and left home by the time they were seven years old anyway.

Even our own parents had it easier, especially in the summer time. Basically, this is what my mom did during the summer. She made us get up and do our chores. Then she let us watch *Let's Make a Deal* while making us bologna sandwiches for lunch. After lunch she made us go outside and hang around with the other neighborhood kids. The boys hung around on one side of the street saying the girls had cooties and the girls hung around on the other side of the street saying we were rubber and they were glue and whatever they said bounced off of us and stuck to them and so forth. Girls always get the best of boys in these types of verbal exchanges, don't you know.

Occasionally, if it was too hot, we went into my best friend's basement and lip-synched our way through her stack of 45's. Our favorite was "These Boots Were Made for Walking." We sang into the ends of her mother's yardsticks while pretending we were wearing black fishnets and white lipstick.

That's how it used to be. We parents of the 1990s, on the other hand, are expected to do all kinds of things for our kids until they leave puberty, which according to the latest U.S. census now lasts until age forty. During the summer, for example, we're supposed to run our kids to five billion classes all day long. In return, they are obligated to teach us computer illiterates how to (a) find a book at the library now that the card catalogues are gone and (b) get to the next board of *Super Mario*.

Of course, the most important thing we as parents are expected to do is to build our children's self-esteem—and that is one task, frankly, I don't mind doing. I was just thinking the other day, however, that it would be kind of nice if we grown-ups could enhance our own self-esteem while we were at it.

"How can I enhance my personal self-esteem?" I asked Ken.

"I thought that's why we have dogs," he said. "You're always telling everyone how smart they make you and me look by comparison."

"Very true," I observed. "You can bet that *we* never leap out of car windows at red lights."

I was, of course, referring to the last time Ken took all three dogs to the groomer's. When he stopped at the light on North Temple and Third West, Basil, who is the (a) youngest and (b) dimmest of the pack, decided to make a run for it, so he jumped out of a partially rolled-up window and legged it over to the Triad Center parking lot where he streaked around like your garden variety greased pig. Ken, naturally, pulled over and proceeded to give chase until he managed to subdue said dog with the aid of three women in high heels who were looking for their car.

"Dogs are great when it comes to making you feel smart," I went on, "but what I want is a pet that will make me feel like a total babe."

"What about another cat?" he said.

I guffawed. "Are you kidding? Cats are the fourteen-year-old girls of the animal kingdom. Pure snots. I've lived with enough cats to know that all they do is sit around all day long and criticize the way you combed your bangs"

"Well, what about a goldfish?"

"Get real," I said. "Goldfish don't even know they're alive let alone that I'm alive."

Which is why, in the end, I decided to buy a cockatiel.

We had a cockatiel when I was growing up. His name was Sam, and he used to do big-time wolf whistles every time my mom and I walked into the room. Needless to say, we thought he was a completely charming bird even though he drew blood anytime someone tried to feed him.

So I went to Western Garden, picked out the bird I thought would be most likely to affirm my babehood, and brought him home. His name is Poirot, and he sits in the corner of my kitchen, whistling his heart out every time we make eye contact, which, as you can imagine, enhances my self-esteem like crazy.

I'm also trying to teach him how to talk. Nothing fancy at first, just a simple "Ann's a babe." If he masters that, we'll move on to slightly more complicated phrases such as "oh, you beautiful doll," as well as "ham and cheese, ham and cheese, Ann's the one with sexy knees."

Naturally, I'd be more than happy to keep you posted on his progress.

Dog on a Diet

*I*t's only a month into the year and already I can tell I'm going to have to admit defeat in the new year's resolution department.

I used to make the same new year's resolution every year. I used to promise myself during the holidays that beginning January 1st I would go on the diet favored by all those guys I knew in high school who used to wrestle in the featherweight division—the one where you have to be forty pounds or under. This diet, known as the PROVO HIGH SCHOOL'S DROP TILL YOU DROP program, was so strict that biting your fingernails or sneaking drinks from the water fountain were considered forms of cheating. No doubt about it, the program was brutal. By the time those kids stopped dieting, they'd not only lost weight, they'd also lost some of their hair and teeth. But hey! They got results! They looked great—as long as they didn't smile—and they were thin. Which is what I would be too once I started dieting after the first of the year, I told myself. Meanwhile I spent December tucking into a cheeseball here and a mince pie there with a minimum of guilt.

Problem was it was always hard to stop doing in January what I had been doing so well for so long. From Halloween until New Year's Day I had eaten like a pro. Eating, in fact, had become my favorite contact sport, and like any dedicated athlete at the pinnacle of her powers, I was loathe to suddenly become a mere spectator, sitting on the sidelines while everyone else was sitting at the table.

Sadly, I have accepted the fact that I am completely incapable of losing weight during the month of January. For this reason, when New Year's rolled around again, I didn't make a resolution to go on a diet. I decided to put my dog Bogie on a diet instead.

Actually, I would have had to make the decision to put Bogie on a diet sooner or later. For a long time now people have been dropping subtle hints about Bogie's bulk. "Gee," they all say, "that little dog of yours sure is fat." Bogie shrugs when he hears this sort of comment. He figures that people are just jealous. Meanwhile he sits on the couch all day long eating pork rinds and watching reruns of *The Love Boat.*

The truth is that eating is the closest thing Bogie ever has to a religious experience. Six times a day he kneels and faces in the direction of the nearest Winchell's. While most people want to be sent to heaven for doing good deeds in this lifetime, Bogie just wants to be sent to Chuck-a-Rama.

Things came to a head one morning right before Christmas, however, when Bogie and I stopped at a gas station to get me a Dr. Pepper after one of our early morning waddles. While I was plunking quarters in the machine out front, Bogie squirted (if a dog of his dimensions can truly be said to squirt) through the gas station door and headed straight for the potato chip rack. At first I was impressed that a dog I had raised from a pup was smart enough to immediately locate the food aisle in a place he'd never been before. But as soon as the service station attendant began to scream and flap his arms around, I came to my senses. I pulled Bogie away from the pretzels, apologized to everyone present, and left with my dog bundled under my arm like so much sausage.

"That does it!" I yelled when we were outside again. "Come January 1st, you're going on a diet!"

Bogie just thought that I was making one of my little jokes, like that time I told him he smells bad when the weather is warm. But I made good on my promise. As soon as the new year started, I put Bogie on a diet. I even gave him a list of fat-fighting suggestions from *Mademoiselle* magazine to assist him in his quest for thinness. They include the following:

* Drink at least eight glasses of water daily.
* Eat your meals from a smaller plate or dog bowl.
* Make eating a pure experience: do not watch TV, read a book, or chase a bicycle while you are chewing your food.
* Imagine how terrific you'll look in a bikini this summer.

I also encouraged Bogie to keep a detailed food diary noting the kinds and amounts of food consumed, as well as his emotional state while eating said food. The idea here was to help Bogie discover destructive behavioral patterns that could be successfully modified.

Well, I just took a look at old Bogie's diary, and I was disheartened to see that he hasn't written down a thing since January 1. Not one word. There are probably a lot of reasons for this, one of which is that Bogie doesn't know how to write. But even if he could write, he wouldn't.

He's way too busy sneaking Oreos when he thinks I'm not looking.

Why I Truly Believe that Cats Are as Stupid as Dogs

After many years of thinking deeply about this sort of thing, I have decided that the world is divided into two types of individuals: (a) dog people and (b) cat people.

People who prefer dogs to cats can be identified by the following traits:

1. They leap on you when you walk through the front door.
2. They jump up on your furniture.
3. They hang their heads out the window when you take them for drives in your car.
4. Their feet twitch when they dream about chasing rabbits.
5. They circle other dog people when they meet in such public places as malls and so forth.

People who prefer cats, on the other hand, can be identified by a single characteristic—i.e., they think they're better than you are, especially if you have dogs.

Indeed, cat people are very fond of telling everybody that (a) dogs are stupid and (b) cats are smart. The proof they offer for this observation is that, whereas a dog will do what you tell it to do, a cat never will.

Cats have minds of their own, don't you know.

Frankly, I have a very difficult time grasping the logic of this argument. It's like saying people who run red lights are actually smarter than people who don't because they're too independent to follow the rules. I went to high school with a girl who routinely ran red lights, and I can promise you that hardly anybody thought this was a sign of high intelligence on her part.

No, I believe cats refuse to do what you tell them to do BECAUSE THEY'RE TOO DENSE TO FIGURE OUT WHAT YOU WANT IN THE FIRST PLACE. Now before you cat-lovers out there take umbrage all over the place, I want to make it perfectly clear that I myself am very fond of cats. I like them at least as much as I like dogs. It's just that I also happen to think they're at least as dumb as dogs although still smarter than cows. I have arrived at this conclusion after spending years in the company of cats.

I've always had at least one cat at any given time, and often I've had more. In fact, my mother's greatest fear is that I'll turn into one of those old ladies with long gray braids and no teeth who has so many stray cats living at my place that A *Current Event* will show up to do a story on me, which will cause all the neighbors to whisper and make mock, thereby forcing my family members to hang their heads in shame and eventually leave town.

The point I'm trying to make is that I have had enough experience with cats to support my views concerning their general intelligence level which I personally do not believe to be high. For instance, when we were kids one of our daily jobs was to follow my dad out to the station wagon and gather up all the kittens, whose names were usually (a) Fred and (b) Barney after the cartoon characters, so that he could back out of the driveway without mowing them down. The reason he worried about running them down was that every time the kittens heard an engine start up, they ran for cover *underneath the car!*

You could see them look at each other, their eyes wide with terror, whenever they heard my dad start the car.

"Oh no!" they squealed at each other. "It's THE NOISE again! Better hide beneath the car!"

Meanwhile they clawed and scratched and bit my brothers and me because we prevented them from seeking safe refuge.

This was not the only experience that led me to believe that cats aren't as bright as everybody says they are. My girlfriend Elise had a Siamese cat named Booby while we were growing up who used to try to go outside by walking through a plate glass window. Since I myself once accidentally attempted to walk through a plate glass window at Trolley Square, I can testify from direct personal experience that it doesn't work. Also nobody gives you a badge telling you how smart you are after you've tried it. Mostly people just stand around staring at you with their mouths wide open while feeling sorry for your caretaker and so forth.

At present we have one cat residing with us. Her name is Cleo, and she spends most of the day chasing her various body parts around the room. Sometimes she chases her tail, sometimes she chases one of her hind legs. Every now and then she catches herself with sharp little teeth, which causes her to yelp and pout.

"Can you believe it?" she whines when I walk into the room. "Like, I was just minding my own business, and, like, somebody actually crept up from behind and bit me." She flips her bangs out of her eyes.

"I'm very sorry to hear that," I say. "Will it make you feel better if we go to the mall together?"

Yes, she purrs, that would be very nice, although she isn't really sure she wants to be seen in public with me.

Would I mind very much, she asks, if I walk ten paces behind her?

Weird Science

Biology Is Destiny

When I was teaching freshman English at Brigham Young University, I received a student paper that said, "After Mendel discovered genetics he was persecuted so much that he ran away to a monastery where he later became a monk." Well, this paper stirred within me a passion for genetics that lasts until this day. Specifically, I am interested in why parents keep passing along their goofy genes instead of their good ones to their offspring. This, to me, is one mystery that science has yet fully to address.

FOR INSTANCE. Although Ken always neatly hangs his towel up after each use, our children naturally inherited the gene from me that makes us drop our towels into steaming little piles on the bathroom floor after we take a shower. What this proves to me is that hanging up bathroom towels is a recessive trait, just like blue eyes and the ability to touch your nose with your tongue at dinner parties.

Our kids have inherited a few undesirable traits from Ken as well. Our oldest son, for instance, inherited The Gene that Makes You a Backseat Driver. Philip is only nine years old, and already he thinks he knows more about driving a car than I do even though (and I can prove this) he never took Driver's Ed. from Mr. Moon at Provo High School like I did. When we go for rides together, Philip sits perched on the edge of the passenger's seat just like a bird dog on point, looking for all the things that I'm doing wrong.

"YOU DON'T NEED TO STOP HERE," he screams into my ear.

"But there's a stop sign," I point out.

"SO?!" he says. "NOBODY'S COMING!"

Gee. I can hardly wait until he's a teenager.

Of course, I inherited a few undesirable traits myself. From my grandmother and her sisters, Bea and Blanche, I inherited The Gene that Makes You Lose Things.

My grandmother and her sisters were always losing things. Once when I took them all on an outing to the mall to exchange pillowcases at Penney's, they lost the take-out lunch we'd just purchased from

Happy Halibut. We were sitting on a bench in the middle of the mall when Bea said, "Blanche, where's our Happy Halibut?"

"I don't know," said Blanche, "Where is it, Bea?"

"I'm asking you, Blanche!" Bea snapped.

"Did you eat it already?" Blanche asked.

"Of course not!" Bea snapped again.

Then Bea and Blanche turned accusing eyes on me and my grandmother.

"Well, we certainly didn't do anything with your Happy Halibut," said my grandmother, deeply affronted.

As it turned out, we were sitting on it. Right there in the middle of the University Mall, we were sitting on four fish fillets and a side of slaw *and we didn't even know it!*

From my mother I inherited the Gene that Makes You Put Strange Things in Containers Where They Don't Belong. My mother is always putting things in unusual containers—jewelry in Tupperware or nylons in Ziploc freezer bags, for instance. Once she and I ordered a gallon of Queen Helene's Liquid Mint Julep Face Mask, and then we put it in some empty Listerene bottles for easy storage. Unfortunately, my dad inherited the Gene that Makes You Think Listerene is in Listerene bottles, which explains why my mother found him spitting liquid all over the bathroom mirror one morning.

"Why were you gargling with my facial, Dear?" she wanted to know.

Actually, my mom and I were always doing this sort of thing to my dad. One night I put my contacts in a glass of water by the sink because I couldn't find their case. During the middle of the night my dad staggered into the bathroom, dropped a couple of Alka-seltzers in the cup, and knocked back my contacts in a matter of seconds. The next morning when we discovered what he had done, my mom and I ran around the house shrieking, beating our breast and asking the cosmos what kind of a man could do something like that to his own daughter.

Ken and I have had similar experiences. Last spring, for instance, I mixed up some root starter in an empty milk carton, then left it standing on the kitchen counter. Ken wandered by and decided he needed a man-sized drink. Well, you can imagine what happened next. He yelled at me and dumped all the root starter down the drain. Then I yelled at him *because* he dumped all my root starter down the drain. Then he yelled back at me because I was more worried about my root starter than I was about him. So I called Poison Control and told them that my husband had gotten into the root starter.

"How old is he?" asked the poisons expert on the other end of the line.

"Old enough to know better," I snapped.

And I really believe that. Ken should realize by now that like my mother before me, I will probably always put things in strange containers. I just can't help myself.

My genes keep getting in the way.

Infectious Disease:
The Gift That Keeps on Giving

I hope Philip doesn't have to write an essay about what he did during his summer vacation when he goes back to school next month. That's because his essay would read something like this:

"In the morning we got up and watched television until 10:30. Then our mom got up to feed us popsicles for breakfast. I wanted banana, but Mom always gave the banana popsicles to my brother Alec. After breakfast we all watched *Perry Mason* reruns on Channel 13 while our mom worked up enough energy to crawl back into bed. As soon as she went upstairs, Alec and I had a fight. He called me Stupid so I called him Stupid back. He kicked me in the stomach so I kicked him in the eye. Alec started it. Then we watched some more TV. At 4:00 it was time for lunch. We had popsicles . . . "

The reason Philip's essay would look like this is that my entire family and I spent the summer quarantined inside our house, trying to get over what certain persons in the medical profession blithely refer to as an "infectious disease."

Actually, this summer has been a very educational experience for me. I have learned a great deal about infectious disease. The main thing I have learned is that there are two kinds—type A and type B. Type A infectious diseases are the viruses that nice polite people who always pay their cable television bill on time get. Examples include cold and flu bugs. These viruses show up at your house wearing white gloves and Sunday hats with the assurance that they'll only stay at your place a day or two before they go next door to infect your neighbor.

Type B viruses, on the other hand, pull up at your house on choppers, dressed in black leather jackets and hobnail boots. The minute they show up, your property value drops, thereby causing the decent people on your street to put up FOR SALE signs in their front yards.

Also the county health department gets wind of what's going on, and before you know it, they send out stout nurses to strap bells around your neck so that everyone will be warned of your imminent approach. Examples of Type B viruses include impetigo, giardia, head lice, pinworms, hepatitis, and certain strains of hoof-and-mouth disease caused by eating food with your feet.

Naturally we all had a Type B virus, although I have been advised by my lawyer, Mr. Mason, not to tell you which one.

Admitting that you have contracted an undesirable disease is almost as embarrassing as losing your slip on Center Street in Provo, which is something I once did while I was talking very loudly to my husband and not paying any particular attention to what my underwear was doing. Still, never let it be said that Ann Cannon does not have a strong sense of *Civic Duty*. Since I have become an authority on antisocial diseases, I gladly entertain the questions that people come to my home to ask (usually after dark) in hopes that they may benefit from my experience. Here are some of the most common queries.

> 1. *How can I tell if I have an unpleasant infectious disease?*
> If you have recently turned any shade of green, yellow, mauve, or taupe, chances are very good (a) that you have an infectious disease and (b) that you will be shunned in polite society for the rest of your life. But don't worry. The good news is that nobody will ask you to donate at the next blood drive.

> 2. *Should I notify the people with whom I have recently come in contact?* Yes, unless you spent the day before you got sick chopping up vegetables for a church dinner. Then you should strongly consider getting on the next flight to South America.

> 3. *How can I live down the experience?* Don't write a column about it.

If there's anything worse than contracting a disease, it's accidentally passing it on to someone you really like. I think this is even worse than sending chain letters to a friend, especially the kind that make veiled death threats such as "IF YOU DO NOT SEND OUT TWENTY COPIES OF THIS LETTER BY MIDNIGHT ON SEPTEMBER 5, 1989, BOTH YOU AND YOUR DOG WILL BE RUN OVER BY A TRAIN!"

Oh, well. We survived the experience. The viruses and their girl-friends got back on their choppers one day and headed for the Million Dollar Cowboy Bar in Jackson Hole, Wyoming.

And if it weren't for the nice little postcards they keep sending us, we'd probably forget they ever visited in the first place.

Back to Biology

*T*he other day as I was wandering through the living room, I happened to notice that our two-year-old son, Geoffrey, was playing the piano with his toes. I couldn't quite make out the tune (possibly a little something from *The Phantom of the Opera*) but I did give him high marks for dramatic interpretation. Also I was interested in the fact that this is an ability which apparently runs in our family.

When my mother was a little girl—and this is the honest truth—she once played the piano with her toes on the *Major Bowles Radio Talent Show*. I used to think this distinction was due to the fact that she grew up in Wyoming where there is a definite shortage of things to do once you've gotten tired of hanging out with the holsteins. I figured Mom hiked in from the pasture one day and said to herself, "Gee, I'm bored. Maybe I'll play an adagio or two with my toes for awhile."

Anyway, I was in the middle of relating all this to my mother and grandmother as we were having the Number Five combo at our favorite Mexican restaurant, when my grandmother suddenly announced she would very much like to see that new movie in town, *Princess Di*. Mom and I shot each other questioning looks because we'd never heard of such a film.

"She has such a sad life, really," my grandmother went on, "having to live with Prince Charles and all."

After considering the matter over chile rellenos for a while, Mom and I figured out that Grandma must mean *The Prince of Tides*—not *Princess Di*.

Now my grandmother didn't mistake the title because she's old or because she doesn't hear well, but rather because she's a female member of our family. Not one of us can get a movie title right to save ourselves. My mother and I, for instance, always refer to that Sigourney Weaver movie *Gorillas in the Mist* as *The Gorilla in Our Midst*, which I personally believe is a much better title anyway.

Quirks like these are genetically transmitted, thereby causing a person to be completely at the mercy of nature in some things. We just can't help ourselves, don't you know, which is why my brothers and I all watch television with our thumbs firmly on the remote control button. It's a family trait. Our dad watches television this way, as did his ancestors before him, flipping through thirty-five channels in sixty seconds or less, driving all their spouses who did not share the same genetic predisposition completely mad.

We do this with radio stations, too, by the way, racing through the call numbers like wildfire in hopes of finding various family members playing the piano with their toes.

I was thinking about this the other day because one of my sons brought home a letter from his school library basically telling us we would all have to go to jail if he didn't *please, please, please* return an overdue book.

"Where is this book?" I demanded. "Did you lose it?"

He gave me a look of disgust. "Duh, Mom. I didn't *lose* it."

"Where is it then?"

He rolled his eyes at how dense I was being. "In my desk."

"YOUR DESK!" I spluttered. "WHAT'S IT DOING IN YOUR DESK?"

He shrugged me an answer, then ran outside to enjoy another terrific afternoon of not returning library books. I felt a stab of guilt as I watched him go. The sad truth is that he comes by this tendency to collect overdue books naturally.

In most areas of my life I am a fairly responsible person as the following list clearly demonstrates.

1. I do not litter.
2. I do not speed in school zones.
3. I do not remove tags from mattresses that don't belong to me.

In these ways, people tell me that I am practically a paragon of public virtue. But when it comes to returning library books on time, I really stink.

In fairness to my mother I must say that she rarely returns books late, and when she does, she marches straight into the library and settles her debt in an expedient and honorable fashion. She would never think of doing what I do all the time—(a) dropping books into the after hours bin at midnight while (b) wearing a disguise thereby causing neighbors to have late night conversations such as the following:

FIRST NEIGHBOR: There goes Ann wearing a moustache.
SECOND NEIGHBOR: Off to return library books again, I see.

So, I've made a New Year's resolution a few months late. From now on MY CHILDREN AND I WILL RETURN OUR BOOKS IN BROAD DAYLIGHT.

And maybe we'll even take them back on time, too!

The Load That Is Laundry

Remember the story about Sisyphus from Greek mythology? He's the Corinthian king who was condemned to roll a big rock uphill for the rest of eternity because he blabbed one of Zeus' secrets around Corinth, namely that Zeus wore a toupee. I can just hear the gods trying to decide what to do with Sisyphus as they lounged around Mt. Olympus one afternoon, sipping nectar and watching the NBA playoffs.

> **ZEUS, KING OF THE GODS**: So what are we going to do with this guy? Nobody mentions my hairline and lives! [Gets up and slamdunks a thunderbolt.]
>
> **POSEIDON, GOD OF THE SEA**: Let's condemn him to watch re-runs of *Gilligan's Island* for the rest of his life!
>
> **HADES, GOD OF THE UNDERWORLD**: I've got an even better idea! Let's make him roll a big rock uphill for the rest of eternity. Now that's my idea of hell.
>
> **DIONYSUS, GOD OF GOOD TIMES**: I'll drink to that!
>
> [Here, the gods all leap to their feet and give each other high fives, thereby causing several major earthquakes up and down the Greek coastline.]

You'll notice that none of the Greek goddesses, who'd gone into Athens for the day to meet for brunch and shop at Nordstrom's half-yearly sale, were around to offer their suggestions. If they'd been present, they would have pointed out that rolling rocks uphill isn't such a bad way to spend a few thousand years. Rolling a rock uphill, for instance, would allow Sisyphus to develop enviable upper body strength as well as work on his tan during the spring and summer months and before you knew it, young Corinthian maidens everywhere would start confusing him with Mel Gibson. No, the goddesses would have argued, if you want to punish the man, make him do his own laundry, including loincloths, for a week.

GODDESSES: Sisyphus, we hereby sentence you to do your own laundry for the period of one week.

SISYPHUS: Oh no! Anything but that! A-a-a-r-g-h! [Jumps off Mt. Olympus, thus leaving his laundry for someone else to do.]

Laundry is the one task that never truly gets done at our house. Sometimes it gets washed. Sometimes it gets folded. Occasionally it even gets put away. But those three things hardly ever happen in the same decade, let alone the same day. Instead this is what usually happens to the laundry at our house. I spend a few hours washing and drying it, and then I heap it unfolded on the couch for a few minutes so I can go make a phone call. Meanwhile my kids immediately invite all their friends over so they can sit on the laundry, then roll in it, and finally start shooting it through the basketball hoop in the corner of our family room. The cat also inspects it to see if perhaps she would like to give birth there so by the time I get off the phone I have to wash everything all over again.

I used to believe I have so much laundry because my kids think it's much easier to toss all their clothes in the hamper at the end of the day rather than to fold them neatly and put them in a dresser drawer. But that alone doesn't explain the sheer tonnage of laundry that greets me whenever I do the wash. That's why I have developed this radical new scientific theory about laundry. (In fact, I am currently awaiting the outcome of a special session of the Utah State Legislature to see if I can get funding for continued research.)

Ann's Theory about Why Household Laundry Appears to Double in Size Every Time You Get Around to Doing It

Laundry is actually a living organism, closely related to the single-celled animal known as the amoeba. Amoebas, as everybody knows by now, will start dividing in two whenever they get bored and can't find anything decent to watch on television, so where there was once one amoeba, now there are fifty hanging out with each other and planning the next family reunion. It is the same with laundry. That's why if you leave a pair of dirty sweatpants in the corner of your bedroom at night, there will be two pair of dirty sweatpants the following morning, and if you don't put those two pair of dirty sweatpants in the washing machine right away, you will have four pair of dirty sweatpants before you've finished reading the morning paper.

This holds true for every item of laundry except socks. If you put a pair of dirty socks in the bedroom corner, there will only be one sock the next day and the mate, who's on its way to South America with all of the money from your top drawer, will never be seen or heard from again. In fact, I'm thinking of going to South America myself.

I only hope someone manages to get my laundry done for me while I'm gone!

My Politeness Problem
(Or the Day I Realized I Had Turned into a New Yorker)

So there I was, illegally parked in a spot with a sign that said U.S. POSTAL SERVICE VEHICLES only.

I knew it was dicey when I parked there, because I have this absolutely huge history of getting caught—just like the one time in my entire life when I parked too close to a fire hydrant and an actual fire truck pulled up just as I was getting out of the car.

Anyway, I was illegally parked there in front of the post office for a grand total of three minutes, and when I came back, sure enough, there was an enormous U.S. Postal Service truck that looked capable of moving heavy machinery penning in my car. Also there were two people in the truck, the driver and his pal, both of them largish guys of the goon variety, who scowled as I approached.

Naturally, my first impulse was to fall on my knees and beg for forgiveness. That's certainly the approach I've always taken. But then I remembered that hey, this was New York after all.

"So," I called to them belligerently, "when are you guys going to get your truck out of my way?"

The two of them came completely uncorked. They told me that I was a such-and-such and that I should go do this and that and I said yeah, yeah, and so on and so forth, and the three of us managed to have ourselves a very satisfying little round of verbal fisticuffs.

That was the moment I realized that after spending nearly a year in their company, I had finally turned into a New Yorker.

New Yorkers pride themselves on their toughness, although after having lived for a time in Finland where the inhabitants think it's just a bunch o' fun to beat themselves with birch branches while roasting in a sauna, I don't think New Yorkers are particularly tough. For my money, there is nothing stoical about the typical New Yorker. The whole notion of a stiff upper lip is completely lost on him. New Yorkers kvetch about everything from the weather to taxes to the Mets.

What they do have plenty of, however, is edge. Get in a New Yorker's face, and he'll get right back in yours.

I remember visiting my sister-in-law while she was living in Manhattan. Whenever a taxi crowded her in a crosswalk, she whipped out an umbrella and cracked it over the hood of the car as though it were an errant Victorian school child.

I, naturally, was totally in awe of this, because according to a friend, I had a problem.

"You're too polite," she said to me. "You have a politeness problem."

While it is true that I once apologized from the delivery table to my o.b. for making so much noise, and while it is likewise true that I once had a lengthy telephone conversation with someone who mistakenly dialed my number and thought I was their cousin, and while it is finally true that my piano teacher still calls me Diane because I'm afraid I'll embarrass her if I point out my true identity, I hardly think of myself as having a politeness problem.

"I'm not *that* polite," I told her. "I do rude things all the time."

"Yeah," she said, "but usually not on purpose."

Great, I thought, so she thinks I'm polite and stupid.

Somewhat shaken, I decided I'd seize the very next opportunity that presented itself to be NOT polite, which occurred when I called the doctor's office. I was put on hold and forced to listen to three entire Neil Diamond songs: (a) "Sweet Caroline," (b) "Cracklin' Rosie," and (c) the stupidest song in the history of the world—i.e., "I Am I Said."

Now, I know that there are a lot of wonderful people out there who love Neil Diamond almost as much as they love Barbra Streisand. Some of my best friends, in fact, are Neil Diamond lovers. It's just that I don't happen to be one of them, so to have to wait on the telephone while listening to Neil whine about no one being there to hear, NOT EVEN THE CHAIR for petessakes, was really more than I could take.

When the receptionist finally picked up my line again, I was firm to the point of brusqueness.

"I really don't mind holding for ten minutes," I said, "but don't you ever dare make me listen to another block of Neil Diamond again."

Then I hung up—after which I promptly called back and apologized.

I don't come by this kind of behavior naturally. Quite the opposite, in fact. I come from a long line of women who, while never aggressive and certainly not mean, could strike true terror in the hearts of lazy sales clerks when the situation warranted it. To this day I can still remember the terse, elegant fit my mother threw when it became apparent that a waitress at our favorite Mexican restaurant had served her boyfriend his Bandido Especial, then lingered lovingly at his table before serving us our combo plates, even though we had ordered months and months before him. It was exactly the kind of fit Jackie O. would have thrown if Jackie O. had had to wait an unreasonable amount of time for her combo plate, too.

So maybe I'm over my politeness problem now that I've butted heads with mail guys. What do you think? I would appreciate your comments very much.

And I promise I'll write you a thank you note as soon as I receive them.

A Good Melon Is Hard to Find

*I*f there's one thing that makes my upper lip sweat for sure, it's trying to pick out a decent watermelon at the grocery store.

My anxiety is caused by the fact that I have a truly terrible track record when it comes to selecting melons. Oh sure. The watermelon I choose at the store may look great hanging around the fruit bin with his buddies like a bunch of bachelors on the *Dating Game*. But when I get him home, I discover that he's just another pretty face whose insides are made of mush, and before I know it I'm swearing I'll never go out with a melon again.

I realize there must be a trick to picking the perfect melon. Every time I walk through the produce department at my favorite grocery store, I see plenty of intelligent-looking people fooling around with watermelons like they know what they're doing. My own mother, who is one of the smartest women I know, likes to check for bee stings because she believes that a watermelon with bee stings will be extra sweet.

I don't know. I realize that next to cows, bees are the world's most stupid creatures, but I find it very hard to believe that they go around stinging watermelons all day long when they could be stinging people instead. Not even cows do that.

Instead of checking for bee stings, most people I've observed at the grocery store spend their time thumping watermelons. Some people thump politely, like they're afraid they might disturb whomever's inside. Other people thump away like they've got a court order to repossess stereos and television sets. I thump, too, whenever the people next to me start up. No use in standing out in a crowd, I always say. Only I have no idea what I'm suppose to be listening for. I guess I must have missed that day in nursery school when they taught us what sound a watermelon makes.

I've been in such a dither about selecting the perfect melon lately that I finally decided to see a fruit expert. I made an appointment to chat about my feelings with the friendly grocer who works in a little market around the corner. Here is a verbatim transcript of our conversation.

> GROCER: So! Your chart here says you've been worrying about watermelons lately. Is that true?
>
> ME: Yes.
>
> GROCER: I see. Do you want to talk about it?
>
> ME [clutching the potato chip rack nervously]: I keep having this recurring nightmare that I go to the grocery store to buy a watermelon for the Cannon family reunion and—and I don't know which one to choose! I see all of those watermelons just staring at me, and then suddenly I realize they're staring at me because I'M NOT WEARING ANY CLOTHES, I'M STANDING IN THE MIDDLE OF SMITH'S PRODUCE SECTION AND I'M TOTALLY NAKED! A-A-A-A-R-R-G-H!!! [Regaining my composure.] I think I need help.
>
> GROCER: I see. Well that's why I'm here. Any questions?
>
> ME: Yes. What qualities do you look for in a melon?
>
> GROCER: Intelligence, physical attractiveness, and a good sense of humor. Ha! Ha! But seriously now--

Well, if there's anything I can't stand, it's a grocer who thinks he's a comedian, and, as a rule, I don't like grocers who think they're therapists either.

The basic problem with watermelons, I've finally decided, is that you can't see what you're buying. They just aren't packaged for the consumer's convenience, so that's why people have to resort to looking for bee stings and thumping and checking their horoscopes closely before making a final selection. In this way the process of choosing a watermelon closely resembles that of choosing a spouse—you really never know what you're getting until you've gotten it.

After years of frustration, not to mention heartbreak, I've finally come up with a foolproof strategy for buying watermelon, and I'd like to pass it on to you. Here it is.

Ann's Famous Rule of Thumb for Buying Watermelon

> Buy any watermelon you damn well please.
> Just make sure you've got your clothes on first.

High-Tech Boots

*B*oy, things sure have changed since I first learned to ski sometime around the dawning of the Mesozoic Era. Back then I had
wooden skis, coiled Miller bindings, and boots with shoelaces. Seriously. I wasn't alone, however. The only people with buckle boots, as
we called them, were (a) hotshots, (b) rich kids, or (c) hotshot rich
kids, and since hardly anyone from Provo BNS (Before Nu-Skin) fit
into one of the above categories, most of us stood around in lift lines,
making small talk and watching our shoelaces freeze.

Actually, I never really took to the skiing thing as a kid. For starters you had to wear all those layers of uncomfortable clothing, including Wonder Bread bags on your feet because someone told your
mother that plastic bags provide good insulation at a great price. The
worst of it was that all those clothes didn't even keep you warm—they
just stopped you from losing assorted body parts to frost bite once you
stepped off the ski school bus.

Of course, that was a big part of the problem—the ski school bus
was so stifling hot you made little puddles of sweat in the bread bags
around your feet. Also you had to sit on the back seat and inhale ex-
haust fumes with your best friend Gigi as the bus fishtailed slowly up
the canyon. This misery was often compounded by the presence of
boys in the seat in front of you who delighted in suggesting in loud
voices that you had cooties and so forth.

Then there's the fact that skiing is such an equipment-intensive
sport. You have to deal with things like poles and boots and skis and
gloves and other things that come in pairs which is a pure nightmare
for certain people like myself who are always losing the mates to their
socks. Also you have to wear goggles—goggles, for petessakes—over
your glasses, thus making you look like one of those alien babies
you're always reading about in the tabloids at the grocery store.

Anyway, the long and short of it is that I pretty much stopped skiing until a few years ago at which point I had to outfit myself all over
again. That's when I noticed the small revolution that's taken place

in the ski equipment industry. That's when I noticed how high-tech everything has become.

I suppose I shouldn't have been so surprised since most things are very high-tech these days. On our last trip, for instance, Ken and I rented a car that actually talked to us, saying snappy car things like "your door is ajar" or "please fasten your seat belts."

"Just what I need," I complained to Ken. "An automobile that nags me."

"I don't think it means to nag you," said Ken, who has an advanced degree in Car Psychology. "I think it just has poorly developed social skills."

As I see it, this broad-based boom in the field of high technology can be attributed directly to the proliferation of computers. Computers are everywhere—in our homes, schools, offices, cars, libraries, grocery stores. It seems like everyone has access to a computer these days, which is why my kids laugh when I tell them what computers were like when I was growing up.

Basically there were two kinds of computers in those days: (a) Big Computers and (b) Robot Computers. Big Computers were very impersonal and large—about the size of a Winnebago—and they were used primarily to launch John Glenn into orbit.

Robot Computers, on the other hand, were much smaller and more personal, which made them ideally suited for television family life. Some of the television families who owned their own robots were the Jetsons, as well as that family on *Lost in Space* who had June Lockhart for a mother. I used to love the way their robot followed the nefarious Dr. Smith around, shouting, "Warning! Warning!" and flapping its arms made out of vacuum attachments.

So as I was saying, I went shopping for new ski equipment and, boy, was I ever amazed! Talk about high-tech. When Ken dragged a pair of boots over for me to try on, I gaped. These boots not only had buckles, but dials and gears and cables and everything else. Truly. You had to be an engineer just to figure out how to put them on your feet, unlike those Wonder bread bags my mother made me wear, which at least had the virtue of being uncomplicated.

"I'm supposed to wear these?" I whined. "I'll look exactly like Robo Cop."

"What are you saying?" Ken asked. "Do you really want to wear lace-up boots again?"

Of course, I shook my head no, then proceeded to ooze myself into the new boots, and by the time I got them on I resembled nobody less than Arnold S. as the Terminator. I felt just like the Terminator, too, utterly invincible, ready to level slopes in a single run. I loved it!

So when the snow flies next year—dare I say something so predictable, so trite . . . "I'll be back!"

The Mysterious Explaining Disease

Ken and I once ended up with a pair of truly great tickets to a Utah Jazz basketball game. They were VIP tickets which basically meant we could (a) mingle and (b) hobnob with other VIP ticket holders in a big buffet room before the game, eating Swedish meatballs and so forth, after which we would take our courtside seats right behind the basketball standard. We had these tickets because someone gave them to someone else who gave them to someone else who finally gave them to us at the very last possible minute.

So, in other words, the tickets weren't really ours.

At least that's how I perceived it. I felt, in fact, exactly like an underaged kid with phony ID. I just knew the moment we tried to pass those VIP tickets off as our own, the person at the gate would look at us and say, "Hold on. These tickets can't possibly belong to the likes of you!" Then he would shout, "Guards, seize them," after which Ken and I would be dragged from the Delta Center by Jazz goons in green coats.

As we approached the ticket taker, I could feel my heart begin to race. When he actually took the tickets from our hands, my upper lip started to sweat. I freely admit it—I couldn't stand up to the pressure.

"Those tickets aren't really ours," I blurted out as Ken's jaw went slack with surprise. And then I launched into the entire explanation of how we had ended up with them.

The ticket taker gave me a tremendously bored look as he shuffled us on our way to the Inner Sanctum of the VIP to the next ticket taker who was also subjected to the entire explanation of why we had such great tickets.

By the time I had told no less than five people we didn't know and would never meet again the true story of The Tickets and How We Got Them, Ken finally said, "Listen to me, Ann. No one cares why we have these tickets. Do you understand me? NO ONE CARES."

It was then I felt the pain one feels when one finally realizes one has been busy embarrassing oneself in public again.

"Actually, you've engaged in this kind of behavior before," Ken later said on our way home from the game. "Remember that time you parked our big family car parallel to the library curb, thereby taking up five spaces? When you realized what you'd done, you personally apologized to every single person in the checkout line for taking up so much room, then explained you'd only done it because you were new in town and didn't yet know all the rules for parking at local libraries?"

"And then there was the time I bought ten copies of the *National Enquirer* for my English students to evaluate in class the next day," I remembered ruefully. "I wanted the clerk to know I was buying them for a legitimate academic purpose, so I explained to her I didn't for a moment really believe that Orrin Hatch is an alien and so forth, and that I was only buying them because I had to."

"I'm sure she believed you," Ken said.

I sighed. "It's a disease all the women in my family suffer from. We have these overactive glands which secrete the hormone responsible for (a) making you feel guilty and (b) wanting to explain yourself to everyone."

There is a very famous story in my family about the time my own mother forgot to wear her glasses on an errand to the bank. While standing in line to cash a check, she saw a man she thought was the family doctor because he appeared to be wearing a white lab coat.

"He kept looking at me," my mother said, "so naturally I started to feel guilty. After awhile I caved in. I marched up to him and told him I was very sorry we hadn't paid our bill yet but that I would certainly take care of it first thing in the morning."

As it turned out, the man wasn't the family doctor.

"Can you imagine how embarrassed I was?" she asked.

In fact, what he said to my mother was (and I quote), "Hey, lady, I'm just a barber."

"Well, it was all his fault," I soothed, "for wearing white in the first place, don't you know."

"So you really think it's a gland thing with you and your mother?" Ken asked.

I nodded vigorously.

"Guys don't have that gland," he said. "I'm pretty sure we learned that in the sixth grade maturation program."

Which may be true. Now that I think about it, I know a lot of women who explain themselves in ways that men would never dream of. One friend, for example, told me that if anyone ever compliments her on an outfit she immediately feels compelled to say, "I bought it on sale at the Rack for $19.99." I'm certain a bunch of guys would never say this sort of thing to one another.

Still, I suspect my mother and I are worse than most women. Like I say, it's a disease—a disease with a long and interesting history.

If you have a minute, I'd just love to tell you all about it.

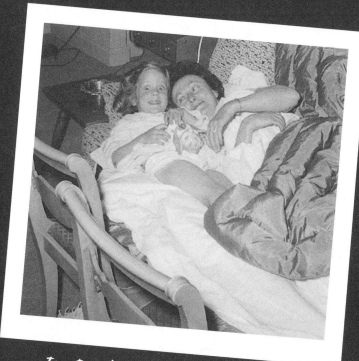

In Praise of Older Women

In Praise of Older Women

The first thing I remember was the day they brought my brother John home from the hospital. He was long and scrawny, this new baby. He didn't talk. He didn't hop. He didn't open and shut his eyes when you wanted him to. He squeaked sometimes, but never on cue. If he had been a toy, I sure wouldn't have asked for him for Christmas.

Only *they* thought he was terrific. They, in fact, draped a blue blanket over a chair, propped John up, and took plenty of pictures. Even though I was not quite three years old, I was embarrassed for my father who kept pulling funny faces for the new baby's benefit. Geez. Talk about not reading your audience.

So I wandered downstairs and tried to get trapped behind the washing machine so someone would have to find me, then tell me how much I had been missed for the last five minutes. When that didn't work, I went outside and stood beneath the crabapple tree, sending telepathic messages to the house such as AN EXTREMELY IMPORTANT PERSON IS STANDING BENEATH THIS CRAB-APPLE TREE. COME ADMIRE HER. IMMEDIATELY.

When that didn't work either, I finally returned to the living room and joined the little group there—my brother, of course, surrounded by my parents and grandparents and great-grandmother, who, with her off-white hair and skin and lovely blouse, seemed the color of cream. I still recall the way her skin hung, light as lace, from her tiny frame.

My great-grandmother, known as Grandma Pat, doesn't occupy center stage of this particular memory, but she's a part of its supporting cast. She was also a part of the company of older women—grandmothers, great aunts, and an assortment of their friends—who spread their wings and hovered over the events of my childhood.

One of my husband's aunts, commenting on the tendency I have to write about these women, lodged a mild complaint with me.

"You always refer to them as *elderly*," she pointed out. "That word has such a negative connotation."

Her point was well taken. I have used the term in connection with my great-aunts whenever I've written about that time they nearly came to blows in the middle of the University Mall for all the world to see because Aunt Blanche accidentally sat down on Aunt Bea's takeout order from Happy Halibut. I would hate people to think, however, that I did not have real affection for them, real regard for their toughness.

That's what I liked best about them, in fact—their toughness. They weren't hard or coarse. In fact, their good manners were ever a perfect complement to their unflagging generosity. But heavens, they were a steely lot!

When I knew her, Grandma Pat had grown quiet and gracefully slow, but make no mistake, I'd heard stories. How she left her husband, changed her name, and headed west to make a happier life for her small son. How she worked for the railroad. How she slept with a shotgun under her pillow. How she shook her fishing pole at a bull in a pasture and dared him to mess with her. How she became game warden in Sublette County, Wyoming. How she stuck her head out the window of a new Model-T and warned folks in the streets they damn well better get out of her way because she didn't know how to stop the car. How she loved beautiful jewelry. How she broke the bank each December making sure everyone in town had Christmas.

My grandmother's oldest sister, Bea, had her tales, too. An inveterate talker, she was interested in everything—*everything*—and could turn a description of her luncheon in the Tiffin Room into a story of Wagnerian proportions. She had other stories, too, memories of horse-drawn sleigh rides at Christmas, of elocution and deportment lessons, of her mother being hauled into court by federal marshalls to reveal the whereabouts of her polygamous husband—tales of an era long passed. Until the day she died, Aunt Bea had the stamina to out-talk, outthink, and outwrite everybody I knew.

My own grandmother was the very toughest of them all. The last time I ever saw her, *she* was bringing in a meal to *me*. And then she cleaned my house afterwards.

Did I hear all their stories? I'm sure I didn't, and even if I did, I probably wasn't listening. Now I can't even ask them what I wish to know most: where did they find their spines? Was it a combination of history and geography that gave these frontier daughters of world wars and the Great Depression their strength? In truth, I feel flabby next to them. A born whiner. Someone who has watched too much television instead of chopping wood.

Still, there are girls coming up behind me now, nieces and daughters of friends. Time for me to be a part of their supporting casts. And if I can't give them exactly the same gifts my old women gave me, at least I can give them some of my own.

Life with Mother

*O*ne thing you could always count on at my mother's house was a darn good Thanksgiving meal.

Turkey, dressing, sweet potatoes, cole slaw, pies—nobody did these things better than Mom. In fact, people came from miles around just to feast at our table, including my grandmother's sisters, who always fought over the biggest drumstick and ended up having rumbles in our kitchen, using hat pins as weapons. Mom's food was that good.

That's why last Thanksgiving came as such a nasty shock.

For the first time in a couple of years we were all together, prepared to (a) give thanks and (b) engage in a serious feeding-type frenzy.

A couple of bites into the meal, however, and we knew we were in big trouble. The turkey was dry, the dressing was soggy, and the rolls came from Albertson's.

It was the rolls that got to me, frankly. Mom didn't even warm them up and try to pass them off as her own, which is what I would have done. Instead she dumped them straight from the plastic bag into a basket right there in front of the whole world, then sat down to eat as though nothing earth-shattering had just happened. So we munched along in stunned silence until my brother who lives in Nevada finally said, "Geez, Mom, this meal really sucks."

"Well," she replied airily, "you do know that I don't cook anymore." That's when my brothers and I knew that our mother had put away her apron and embarked (once again) on a new lifetime.

Unlike most children, who assume that their mothers were never anything than what they are now, we knew perfectly well that Mom had been another person altogether before she decided to study for the Donna Reedhood and have us. We had this information firsthand from the people who watched her grow up.

Mom is from Wyoming, a very cow-intensive region of the country, so we often spent our summers in her hometown, hanging around Grandpa's gas station and watching bovines in action. In fact, we became the ultimate authorities on cow behavior and plan to write a book soon called *Cattle in the Mist*.

Anyway, what we learned basically is that cows are the dumbest things in the universe. If you honk at one standing in the middle of the road, for example, it won't occur to her that you want her to shake her haunches and move. No. She just thinks you're flirting, and the next thing you know your car is going out on a date with her.

But I digress.

The *really* interesting things we learned during those summers were about our Mom. People would stroll into the garage and say to my grandpa, "These Patti Lou's kids?"

Grandpa would nod yes. "Too bad she married that fellow from—*spit*—Utah."

(Here's something else we learned: people from Wyoming hate people from Utah because they think we're wimps to which I can only say at least the men down here don't wear shoes with pointy toes.)

Then these individuals would turn to us and say, "I remember the day your mother did—"

Our mother did all sorts of amazing and wonderful things—pump gas while shampooing her hair, challenge the school bully to a fight because he wouldn't stop picking on a weaker classmate, race through town in my grandpa's Cadillac, kicking up gravel and dirt. But best of all she was once rodeo queen.

There aren't many people who can say that about their mothers when you stop to think about it.

We liked to imagine how she must have looked wearing a tiara on the brim of a smart stetson, riding horseback around the ring while alternately doing stunts and saluting the cheering crowd. So different from the pretty mother who kept us clean and made us eat mush in the morning and worried that we might do something dangerous.

Who made us feel that we were the center of the universe.

Obviously we're still important to her, but we're gone now, and she decided it was time for another incarnation so she stopped cooking and started studying. She's a full-time student, something she's always wanted to be, majoring in humanities. These days, when I talk to her on the phone, she drops names like Plato all over the place.

So at every Thanksgiving time from now on, I know that while I won't be able to give thanks for her homemade rolls, I am deeply grateful for her example. She's taught me that life is not one but a series of personal odysseys.

God bless her always.

The Red Bag

My grandmother and I often worked at cross purposes: I would put things out for the Deseret Industries truck; she would whisk them off my front porch and put them back on my shelves because I might need them later. She would bring over fried chicken for lunch; I would tell her that I had already fixed us some tuna sandwiches. That's the way it was with us. We loved each other, but we drove each other crazy.

She was a woman who took profound delight in the company of very young people, my grandmother. Perhaps because the memory of her own Cache Valley girlhood was ever fresh with her, she understood children utterly—their fears, their triumphs, their rages, their pleasures. And she also understood what small children want the adults in their lives to provide.

I can remember crawling into her bed long before the sun was up where I chattered away like a noisy little bird as she listened to me, interrupting occasionally to ask the kinds of questions people ask when they are really paying attention to you, and when she laughed, it was always in the right places. Sometimes she told me her growing-up stories—how she'd loved playing softball with her brother and swimming in the icy waters of Bear Lake. How she'd hated her freckles and rubbed a special preparation on them to make them disappear. How she'd wanted Santa to leave her a doll with a china head for Christmas one year.

She was particularly gifted at providing the kinds of small physical attentions children savor—she would scratch my back for hours as I watched cartoons in the afternoon, and when night fell, she provided warm milk laced with honey, as well as flannel quilts and pillows sheathed in crisply cool pillowcases. She relished, in fact, all the little jobs of maintaining children—brushing hair, filling up the bathtub, getting out the toothbrush.

One morning when we were outside, my grandmother told me that trees had their own secret language.

"Can you understand them?" I asked her.

"Yes," she said. And then she translated.

My grandmother loved me hugely when I was little, and I loved her back.

As I grew older, however, things between us became more complicated. Eager to prove to the world that I could take care of myself, thank you very much, I began to find her attentions annoying. By the time I was a teenager, they even felt intrusive—like attempts to control me.

"I'm not a baby anymore," I would whine to my mother. "Grandma treats me like a baby."

Even after I was married with babies of my own, my grandmother hovered—advising me how to eat and what to wear when the weather turned raw—and I responded sullenly, assuming that her remarks were implied criticisms of the way I was running my life.

Sometimes I would watch her with adults who weren't members of the family and marvel at how wonderful she was with them. Warm and wise, interested and intelligent—she inspired genuine, lasting affection. She kept in close and constant touch with women she had known for fifty years.

There were those times when the two of us would come together in a grown-up friendship, too. We'd compare plans for our gardens, for instance, while sipping sodas and sitting outside to enjoy the breeze. Peers. Comfortable in one another's company. But then she'd start fussing—had I read that article on what too much sun could do to my skin? Did I know that laundry detergent was on sale at Sears and should she place an order for me? That's when I would turn as mulish as a teenage girl in love with the wrong boy, digging in my heels and refusing to turn from my course of action.

Whenever I would complain about the ways my grandmother interfered, friends would look at me like I was crazy. "How can you whine about a woman who brings Jell-O salads and cleans up your house every time she comes to visit?"

"She brings salads because she thinks my children are starving to death," I would tell them. "She cleans up the house because she thinks I won't do it myself."

One of those friends eventually told me to grow up. "So she doesn't do what you want her to do. Get over it. Give her some space."

This really stung. After all, *I* wasn't the one giving my grandmother suggestions for improvement every time she turned around. Excuse me, but *I* wasn't the one trying to change *her*. When I pointed out these things to my friend, she shrugged.

"She doesn't think you're incompetent. She gives you advice because she wants to be important to you."

Which, I grew to understand, was the truth. My grandmother had a hard time accepting the fact that the children she'd loved so much—my mother, my brothers, me—had changed into people she hardly recognized. She worried, I think, that once we put childhood behind us, we would cease to need her, not realizing that we needed her still, only after a different fashion.

And so she continued to tell me what to do and I continued to ignore her suggestions. But I listened, at least, and I was usually kind. Whenever we ended one of our conversations, she told me that she loved me, and I told her that I loved her.

The red bag, however, stirred up all my old resentments. The night before we left for our year in New York, my grandmother showed up with an old red leather bag.

"Do you have a first-aid kit?" she asked.

I shook my head no.

"I knew you wouldn't, so I put one together for you." She handed me the red bag stuffed full of bandages, Tylenol, Neosporin cream, cottonballs, and rubbing alcohol.

I was tired. I was hypersensitive. I said I didn't have room for one more thing. I gave her back the bag. She said I was tired. She said I was hypersensitive. She said of course I had room for a first-aid kit. She gave me back the bag.

"That damn bag!" I spluttered later to my husband. "It's a symbol of my entire adult relationship with Grandma."

The petty part of me wanted to leave the bag behind, but in the end I stuffed it somewhere in the back of the U-Haul and promptly forgot about it.

Several months after we left Salt Lake City, my grandmother became gravely ill. Six weeks later she died.

Not long after her death, my son Dylan sliced his finger open. "I need a band-aid," he cried. "I need a band-aid."

Since a band-aid is the only thing rarer at our house than a library book that isn't overdue, I told Dylan we would have to stop the blood flow with napkins from Little Caesar's. But then I remembered: I had a first aid kit, a really nifty one with band-aids and ointment, too, a gift from Grandma across time and miles with no strings attached.

Not long ago I had a dream. I dreamed I walked into a room and found her sitting in a chair.

"I've been wondering when you would show up," I told her. "I've been busy," she said. "You know me."

"Yes," I said.

And then we walked outside into the white hot sunlight. The grass was green and steaming, and the branches overhead were filled with glossy birds who—I'm not joking—were chanting African folk songs.

Unrushed, my grandmother and I linked our arms and listened to them, enjoying their fine and unexpected performance.

And So On and So Forth

Wimps Need Not Apply

I thought I had a pretty good idea before Ken and I got married about the kinds of things that couples usually fight over—money, kids, in-laws, toothpaste tubes, and toilet lids. I knew so much because I took an Achieving Success in Marriage class while we were engaged. Also I've been reading Ann Landers since I was nine. So naturally I figured I had the causes of marital discord pretty well pegged.

That is until I took my first vacation with my (then) new husband and his family.

Here was my family's idea of vacation. First of all, we loaded up the old station wagon with plenty of Cheezits and Snickers bars. Then we all got in and drove to some place hot—Southern California, Arizona, or (in a pinch) St. George. We found a motel that had the following five items in order to meet our rigorous standards:

1. A television.
2. A swimming pool.
3. A drink machine.
4. An ice machine.
5. Magic Fingers.

This set-up was pretty much our collective idea of heaven, especially if the place also came with heavy black drapes that you could draw shut until 1:00 in the afternoon which seemed like a pretty good hour for most of us to roll out of bed. Once we rolled out of bed, we turned on the TV set and watched *Donahue* or *Star Trek* reruns while we scrounged around for a towel and some thongs. Then we all schlepped around the pool for the rest of the day, making periodic trips to the drink and ice machines. Sometimes my dad left for awhile to go buy us some more Cheezits. At night we all went out and had pizza. In my mind, that was a vacation, and I figured everyone did vacations more or less the same way.

Not so.

Let me tell you about my first vacation with Ken's family. Ken's family decided it would be fun to go some place cold—Bryce Canyon in the middle of winter no less. And instead of loading up their cars with junk food and crossword puzzle magazines, they strapped cross-country skis and poles to the roofs of their cars. We drove to Ruby's Inn at the mouth of Bryce Canyon and checked into rooms with kitchenettes which Ken's family stocked with food from all four of the basic food groups after Ken's mom first cleaned the fridge. Then everybody woke up at six the next morning and got ready to ski for fourteen hours. "What do we do now," I asked that night as I dragged my body through the doorway. "Have a yodeling contest?" Until I married Ken, I had no idea a person had to be in basic training just to survive a vacation. I had no idea, in fact, that there is a variety of vacation for which wimps need not apply.

The real problem with traveling with the active person is that you have to take along a lot of paraphernalia. For example, all I need on a vacation is a swimming suit and a pair of thongs. And if I forget the thongs, I can always buy a new pair at a Payless somewhere. Active people, on the other hand, can't leave home unless they take at least five different kinds of foot gear with them—running shoes, tennis shoes, golf shoes, hiking boots, and waders. They also take along binoculars, field guides, fishing rods, and video cameras to record how much fun they're having. Sometimes Ken even likes to take along a steam iron—just in case we get in the mood to do his shirts while we're gone.

Ultimately this difference in vacationing styles boils down to a fundamental difference in philosophy. One group of people thinks a vacation ought to improve them in some way—culturally, physically, intellectually, or socially. They think a vacation ought to broaden their horizons, not just their hips, and they attack each day as though they were storming a hill. Rambos of Leisure I like to call them. This, of course, is just the opposite of the other group, which basically wants to slide a few rungs down the old Evolutionary Ladder and see what it feels like to be an amoeba for awhile.

Still, things aren't entirely hopeless. An amoeba married to a Rambo can learn to get along. Over the past twelve years, for instance, Ken and I have perfected the art of compromise—I'll climb a mountain with him if he'll eat something unhealthy with me afterwards. Sometimes we even switch places. On a trip to Jackson Hole last summer, the fresh air must have done goofy things to me because I suggested we go for an early morning bike ride. Ken looked at me, smiled feebly, and said we'd have to do it later in the day.

He wasn't getting out of bed before noon.

Travel with Family

When my brothers and I were teenagers, we spent an entire summer travelling across these United States with our parents, and do you know what we remember most? The birthplace of Abraham Lincoln? The White House? The Statue of Liberty? The bayous of Louisiana?

No.

What we remember most is that one night in Toledo, Ohio, our mother ate an entire pepperoni and sausage pizza *by herself* in the motel room while the rest of us went out to buy soft drinks. When we came back, we found her sitting on a bed with an empty pizza carton, doing crossword puzzles and watching Columbo on television.

"DID YOU EAT ALL THAT PIZZA BY YOURSELF?" we screamed at her. "Of course not," she said.

And to this very day she denies that she actually ate her family's dinner when they were out roaming the streets of Toledo, trying to scare up a few crummy beverages.

The memory of that night still rankles.

This experience, and others not unlike it, have led me to the conclusion that what families do best on summer vacations is get on each other's nerves. For instance, my brothers and I frequently had conversations in the back seat of our old station wagon that went like this:

"Stop breathing like that."

"Like what?"

"Like that. You're doing it on purpose to bother me."

"No, I'm not." (Breathe, breathe, breathe.)

There were plenty of variations on this theme.

"Your foot is touching me."

"No, it's not."

"Yes, it is."

"No, it's not."

"Mom, John's foot is touching me."

"It's not my foot, duh, it's my *anklebone*!" (Touch, touch, touch.)

Occasionally, we stopped thinking of ways to bug each other and focused instead on ways to annoy our parents. Whenever Mom and I went into a public restroom together, for instance, I made sure I touched the faucets with my bare hands in front of her because it made her so crazy. My mother just hates to touch anything in public restrooms, so she does things like kicking doors open with her feet, which makes the experience of going into a restroom with her a lot like going into a restroom with a highly trained SWAT team. Whenever Mom and I enter after she's busted down another bathroom door, I want to yell, "FREEZE! YOU'RE UNDER ARREST!" to all those startled ladies washing their hands.

Of course our parents always got back at us. My mother denied she'd eaten our pizza, for example, while my father always lied to us about the interesting and educational things he'd seen while we were napping in the backseat. Once he came out of the men's restroom at a service station in Winnemucca and told us that there were magic toilets in there.

"Magic toilets?" we all said, our eyes agog.

"Yes," said my dad, "all you have to do is point at the toilet and say, 'One, two, three, flush!' and then it just flushes all by itself. Magic!"

Well, we said he was lying, and he said he wasn't, which drove us all completely nuts because he seemed so sincere, and by the time we got to San Francisco, he had us kids convinced that there really were magic toilets in Winnemucca which is something I still believe with all my heart.

Ken's family also drove each other crazy on vacations, especially when they had to go boating on the Great Salt Lake with their Uncle Mel. Uncle Mel had a houseboat that he maneuvered around the lake at speeds approaching 1.8 mph which gave everybody plenty of time to get on each other's nerves. Every now and then Uncle Mel would say, "Hey, why don't we open this baby up!" He made Ken and his sisters put on life jackets and then proceeded to crank up the houseboat to speeds hovering near 3, sometimes 4 mph. Ken and his sisters used to sit on the deck, breathing through their mouths instead of their noses so they wouldn't have to smell the lake, muttering things like, "Boy, we wish we'd never been born," or "Boy, we wish Uncle Mel had never been born." To this very day Ken can't understand why all those German tourists wearing backpacks and black socks with their sandals want to visit the Great Salt Lake whenever they blow into town.

Uncle Mel, on the other hand, is more than happy to give them all the ride of their lives.

Resolutions

I recently found a diary I kept when I was ten years old, and I was interested to see my list of New Year's resolutions on the inside cover.

They follow:

1. BE PATIENT.
2. DON'T TALK ON THE TELEPHONE TOO LONG.
3. BE NICE TO ALL MY FRIENDS.
4. BE A GOOD STUDENT.
5. DON'T SHOW OFF LIKE PEGGY MOORE. (Author's note: Peggy Moore was a very snotty fourth-grade girl who thought she was better than everybody else just because she wore a real bra.)
6. DON'T SWEAR OR SPIT.

About half way through the year I apparently did a little self-evaluation because penciled in the margin next to each resolution are the words (a) "needs work," or (b) "needs more work," or (c) "needs a lot more work." In fact, I probably ought to be working on them still, although it is true that I no longer spit at my brothers when we get into fights. Also, even though I now have a real bra just like Peggy Moore's, I never brag about it.

The problem with my old list, as I look at it, is that I set myself up for failure. I had no idea how to set realistic goals, and thus ended up feeling frustrated and incompetent, which dramatically lowered my self-esteem and so forth. Therefore, these days I only set goals that are manageable, goals I know I can attain with a little discipline and perseverance.

Well, now that we're well into the new year, it's time to check up on this year's batch of resolutions:

1. DO NOT CLEAN OUT MY CLOSET: A
2. DO NOT PAY OFF VISA: A
3. DO NOT START A REGULAR EXERCISE PROGRAM: A

4. DO NOT TAKE UP A NEW HOBBY: A
5. DO NOT IMPROVE MY MIND: A+
Yes! And it's another great report card!

See? Setting and realizing a goal is a snap once you know how. Actually, I came dangerously close to making a genuine resolution this year. Here's what happened. Right before Christmas I stood in a Payless checkout line behind a woman who was packing an infant around in a carrier on her back. Now I have the exact same model as she did, but whereas mine is dirty and dingy, hers was crisp and clean.

I tapped her on the shoulder. "Doesn't your baby ever spit up?" I asked her politely.

She regarded me, a complete stranger, coldly. "Excuse me?" "Your carrier looks brand new. Mine looks—you know—totally gross." I tossed off one of those airy laughs you're always reading about.

"Well," she said, "I clean mine." Then she started to inch away from me.

Suddenly I felt just like I did that time Dylan swallowed some staples, and I had to tell the emergency room nurse that he was one shot behind on his immunizations.

"Okay fine," I said to the nurse who pursed her lips, then scribbled away on Dylan's chart. "You just go right ahead and put down that his mother is white trash."

It is true that I have this huge streak of white-trashiness, and although it doesn't usually bother me, sometimes I get the urge to do something about it, which I did right there at Payless. I shook and turned red in the face and silently swore that from now on I would be a paragon of middle-class virtue and that I and all my possessions would be completely respectable.

Of course, by the time I got to the parking lot, I was feeling much better, so I downgraded my resolution a little, then added it to my list:

NEVER ASK STRANGERS IF THEIR BABIES SPIT UP.

Bonus!!! Cosmo-type Personality Quiz!!!

In case you are wondering about your own personal level of white-trashiness, I have developed this quiz for you.

1. Grease and salt are two of my favorite foods.
   YES NO

2. I have empty pop cans rolling around in my car.
   YES NO

3. There are Big Wheels on my front porch at all times.
   YES NO

4. I have also had a large household appliance such as a broken washing machine sitting on my front porch overnight at one time or another.
   YES NO

5. Twinkies are another of my favorite foods.
   YES NO

6. My children sometimes wear socks to bed.
   YES NO

7. I leave my Christmas lights up until the Fourth of July.
   YES NO

Scoring Your Quiz

—If you answered NO to all of the questions, you are no doubt the lady I stood next to at Payless.

—If you answered YES to some of the questions, don't worry. No one will ever know about your tendencies unless you choose to show them your answers.

—If you answered YES to all of the questions, take off your shoes, grab a tub of bar-b-que curly fries at the drive-in nearest you, and come on over to my house. I'll be waiting!

More Resolutions

On January 1st our eight-year-old-son, Dylan, decided to try his hand at making New Year's resolutions. Later that day as I was picking up stray newspapers, old *TV Guides*, and Smith's cheese ball wrappers from the floor, I found his list. These were Dylan's goals for the year:

    1. DRINK MORE PEPSI.
    2. BUY MORE BASEBALL CARDS.

As you can imagine, I was very impressed with my young son. What a terribly clever boy, I thought, to set goals for himself *that he might actually reach!*

I don't mind telling you that I was inspired, and I decided right then and there to make up generic lists of resolutions that will positively guarantee success for individuals from all walks of life. I pass these along to you, the reading public, absolutely free of charge.

New Year's Resolutions for Guys
    Do not stop for directions.
    Do blame other people for losing the remote control.

New Year's Resolutions for Women
    Do obsess about your hair.
    Do ask other people what you should do with your hair.
    Do not believe other people when they tell you your hair
        looks fine the way it is.

New Year's Resolutions for Fourteen-year-old Boys
    Do not wear a coat in the middle of winter.

New Year's Resolutions for Fourteen-year-old Girls
    Do not, under any circumstances, be seen in public with
        your mother.

New Year's Resolutions for Ten-year-old Boys
    Do lie regularly when asked about brushing your teeth.

New Year's Resolutions for Babies
Do take your socks off in the checkout line at Albertson's.
Do stick your fingers in people's mouths while they are
talking.

New Year's Resolutions for Dogs
Do sit on the furniture when nobody is looking.

New Year's Resolutions for Cats
Absolutely do not do anything you don't want to do.

I had so much fun writing resolutions for everyone else that I went off the deep end and actually wrote some *for myself.*

As you already know, I make it a strict practice to avoid self-improvement schemes, primarily because I'm not very good at them. Still, I decided it was finally time to get serious about an exercise program. Yes, it was time for me to firm up and thereby get in touch with my Inner Babe.

True, it had been a few years since I embarked on a regular fitness program. The last time was in Miss Erkanbrack's seventh grade gym class where we were required to do exercises to "You and Me" by the Turtles every day after roll call. Even after all these years, whenever I hear the words to that song—"Me and you and you and me, no matter how they tossed the dice/ It had to be"—I immediately start doing (a) jumping jacks followed closely by (b) squat thrusts. This can prove to be somewhat embarrassing if I am listening to Musak in places such as grocery stores or crowded elevators.

Still, I was undaunted, and I decided to get started on my new fitness regime by watching one of those morning exercise shows I'd heard they have on ESPN. I pulled on my sweats, turned on my TV—and gasped. I could tell right away that I would never succeed because I simply do not have the right accessories to exercise in the 1990s:

1. I do not have a wide black belt to cinch around my waist.
2. I do not have a gadget to monitor my heart and pulse rate
   to strap onto the belt which I do not have.
3. I do not have a head mike.

It was the head mikes that got to me. Here were all these very young, very buff looking men and women standing mere inches apart, and they were all communicating with one another *via their head mikes*. It was like watching Janet Jackson in concert.

Actually, I've been seeing a lot of head mikes around lately. There's that new television commercial with Kathleen Sullivan in a chopper, for instance, who tells us all about Weight Watchers through her head mike while she's busy buzzing pedestrians below.

Also the managers at the McDonald's where I always go to lunch wear head mikes. They dash about like secret service men guarding the president along a parade route. It's pretty impressive to watch, actually, although I haven't noticed that I get my All-American meal any faster than I used to.

So anyway I've given up the exercise thing for now because I don't have a head mike and probably never will—I guess my Inner Babe will just have to wait.

Haughty Beauty

*W*inter is not a good time for me. Each year the combination of pale days and cold nights nearly does me in. In short, I get the blues. Knowing this, a friend of mine tried to cheer me up recently.

"What you need," she said, "is a good book. Nothing high-minded. Nothing serious. Just pure escape literature."

I told her that I already had a shelf full of cozy murder mysteries featuring lots of homicidal old British people who like to garden in their spare time.

She stared at me. "No wonder you're depressed," she said. "What you need is a little historical romance in your life."

"Historical romance?" I said. "You mean like Victoria Holt and Mary Stewart?" I remembered the books I'd read in junior high school about plain but spunky governesses serving moody masters in spooky mansions.

My friend let rip with a mighty snort. "Hey, forget Victoria Holt," she said. "It's time you graduated to bodice-rippers." And before I knew it, my friend had me in tow at B. Dalton's where she and I perused the Romantic Fiction section. The books had titles like *Tame the Wild Heart*, *This Fierce Splendor*, and *Texas Spitfire*. The covers all featured couples in a clinch. The women had lots of hair ("manes" my friend told me) and gauzy blouses undone to there. The men, all of them shirtless, looked like they did laps together every day at the gym.

"Here's how these books work," said my friend. "The man is virile and arrogant. The woman is beautiful and haughty. Naturally there are lots of fireworks when the two come together."

"Naturally," I said. I picked up a book called *Texas Captive* and read the jacket. "Victor Maurier had sworn never to trust a woman. Then he glimpsed the nubile nymph that frolicked in the dappled sun and the hot-blooded man instinctively knew this exotic sprite was in a class of her own."

"Nubile nymph?" I said. "Exotic sprite? Who are these people?" Already I knew I liked the spinsters in my murder mysteries better, even though they sometimes slipped each other a little digitalis in their tea cups.

"How about this one?" asked my friend, holding a book titled *Silver Rose*. She read the cover copy to me. "When she fled Wyoming to escape her lecherous boss, golden-haired Silver Dupres was sure she'd be safe disguised as a boy on an expedition to chart the Colorado River. Then she gazed at the explorer's rugged, towering scout, and her powerful response reminded her full force how much of a woman she was . . ."

I looked at the cover. Silver and Scout were grappling in a canoe like a couple of wrestlers.

"I guess the disguise didn't work," I said.

"Well," said my friend, "here's one called *River Temptress*."

I read the jacket cover. "Rugged Louis Saint-Denis had journeyed from Louisiana all the way to Mexico, intent on succeeding in his daring mission for France. Then he met the restless, ripe Manuela . . ."

"Oh please," I said.

In the end I bought a book just so that I wouldn't hurt my friend's feelings—*The Raider* by Jude Deveraux—and I read all 346 of its steamy pages in a single sitting. While I can't say it is the best book I've ever read, it certainly has given me a new way of looking at things. Indeed, *The Raider* has helped me redefine what I want to do with my life. I've decided that one day I'd like to be a Haughty Beauty—just like proud-tempered Jessica Taggert. I'm working on a resume now that looks something like this:

NAME: Ann Edwards Cannon
EYES: Sea-mist blue
HAIR: Ebon
VITAL STATISTICS: 15 pounds too ripe
SPECIAL SKILLS: Flaring my nostrils, tossing my ebon mane, lifting my chin defiantly, making saucy retorts, storming from rooms, slamming doors behind me, driving arrogant men wild.
REFERENCES AVAILABLE UPON REQUEST.

I can see it now. With resume in hand, I go to interview for a position as a junior high school English teacher. The principal, a proud man named Deke de Wilde, walks into the reception area. Our eyes lock. I lift my chin. He narrows his eyes into hard yet appreciative slits. I notice he isn't wearing a shirt. Maybe he forgot to pick it up at the cleaners, I think.

"So," he says with an insolent drawl, "you think you can teach seventh graders to diagram a sentence, do you?"

My eyes blaze. I quiver with outrage. But it's no use. In the end I know that passion will claim us both—on the wild frontiers of public education!

Why I Love the Soaps

*N*ow that summer is really gone for good, I can get back to the serious business of watching soaps.

There was a time when I would have denied that I watch daytime television. "Me watch *One Life to Live*? Surely you jest. I'd rather read important novels or listen to a tuba concerto," I'd say. But then I'd accidentally give myself away. I'd overhear a couple of clerks at Smith's Food King discussing *Santa Barbara*, for instance, and before I knew it I'd be yelling down the aisle, "Hey, what gives with Mason and Julia these days?"

So I've decided to go public. 'Fess up. Tell the truth. I've loved the soaps ever since my grade school days when I first thrilled to the moody strains of the *Dark Shadows* theme song.

Over the last twenty years I've sampled most of the soaps on television at one time or another. I even watched the *Edge of Night* for a little while and admit to that only because I read somewhere that Bette Davis watched it too. I assume that she and I and my Aunt Bea were the only people in America watching before the network indulged in a little mercy killing and pulled the plug on the series.

No matter. *Edge of Night*, *General Hospital*, *All My Children*—I've watched them all for the same reason. The characters may be shallow, self-absorbed, and silly, but they certainly lead more interesting lives than I do, especially during the fall and winter months.

Think about it. When was the last time you got stuck in a monastery with a really swell-looking monk. But that's exactly what happened to Hope Brady on *Days of Our Lives*. Hope found it necessary to hide out for awhile with Brother Francis, a former All-American quarterback blessed with superior chest definition. Because Hope didn't have a change of clothes handy, Brother Francis nipped like a good Christian into the catacombs and returned with a strapless sequined party dress—just the sort of thing that gets donated to monasteries all the time I'm sure. Hope put on the gown and promptly turned into a bosomy vision of loveliness. Poor Brother Francis! What's a good monk to do?

Now that's the sort of the thing that never happens to me. For starters I don't own a party dress. Also I don't know any monks. Of course maybe interesting things would happen to me too if I had an exotic name with three syllables like Savannah, Felicia, Augusta, or Santana. Maybe if I had a name like that, foreign agents would chase me around Stockholm or Trinidad, too. Not surprisingly, soap opera women date soap opera men who also have interesting names. Buzz, Cruz, Scorpio, Dakota, Roman (as in Ben Hur), Zed, and Zane—you figure right away guys with names like these (a) know karate and (b) hunt big game in their spare time.

Naturally these people look good, even after having babies in elevators. The men have teeth and hair to spare. And the women? Well, suffice it to say that none of them would wear sweatsuits from Sears like I do, not even to their spas or health clubs. No. These ladies have turned good grooming into high art. What long nails, what clearly defined brows, what small pores they all have! I like their earrings best, though. I don't know anybody in real life who has to remove an earring just to talk on the phone. Do you? Nobody I know in real life has earrings that big. But call your favorite soap star on the telephone and she'll start grabbing her ear just like she's Joan Collins on *Dynasty*.

What I like very best, however, are the interesting things soap characters get to say to one another. While I spend most of my days saying things like "stop feeding your sandwich to the dog" or "what do you mean you got another parking ticket," soap characters get to say things like "can you prove he isn't really Victor's child?" How I would love to flare my nostrils and shout along with Victoria Buchanan that I too have been to hell and back. Or exclaim just like Lars Englund, "I'm not a fugitive! I'm a dancer! And I gotta dance!" This is classic stuff. So are certain lines that show up over and over again. "Is that a threat?" a character will ask. "No," another snaps, jaw muscle twitching, "that's a promise!" My personal favorite, however, is the line that good-looking unmarried soap people use on each other all the time. "I want you," they say. And who can blame them?

Certainly not me. So, Brother Francis, if you're out there somewhere, listen to me: I want you.

Christmas Cheers

Pregnant Ho! Ho! Ho!

*I*n the splendid cathedral at Chartres, France, there is a piece of medieval statuary depicting the Holy Family shortly after the birth of the baby Jesus. Mary, in sensible French fashion, is lying down looking lovingly at the child by her side, while Joseph is gently draping another blanket across the legs of his tired but very pleased wife. A small donkey and an ox look on.

The scene, although shaped in stone, is surprisingly warm.

Philip, who was four years old that spring we lived in Europe, viewed it with great interest.

"Who's this?" I quizzed, pointing to the tightly swaddled infant.

"Baby Jesus," he answered.

"Who's the woman?" I continued.

"Mary," he replied.

"And who's the man?" Philip scrunched up his face in thought. Then it suddenly brightened, like the sun breaking away from a cloud. "I know!" he shouted. "The doctor!"

Although Philip was only four, he was old enough to understand that his own mother is more or less in favor of having a doctor on hand whenever she gives birth, and he figured Mary probably felt the same way. Actually, Mary probably did feel the same way, but the circumstances of her labor and delivery were, in a word, unusual.

I've been thinking about Mary a great deal this holiday season because, as everyone who has bumped into me lately knows, I am hugely pregnant.

During Queen Victoria's reign, being pregnant really meant something. It meant that you got to stay home, put your feet up, and watch soap operas written by Charles Dickens on television all day long. It was great. The reason Victorians treated pregnant women this way was that Queen Victoria was the one making up all the rules then, and she knew from direct personal experience that deep in their hearts, pregnant women would rather be lounging around the conservatory munching on Wheat Thins than doing Jane Fonda's workout tape for expectant mothers.

Today's pregnant woman, on the other hand, isn't even supposed to feel pregnant. She isn't supposed to feel weak or nauseated or short of breath or ready for bed every night by 7:30. Also she's supposed to run in southern Utah's St. George marathon the day before she gives birth. The twentieth-century woman isn't supposed to feel pregnant because it has been scientifically proven by the American Academy of Talk Show Hosts that there are NO TRUE DIFFERENCES BETWEEN THE SEXES, and since men don't feel pregnant, women can't either. Just remember that the modern rule of thumb for dealing with a pregnant woman who says her back hurts because she's been packing around twenty-five extra pounds of kid all day long is to tell her she's making it up. She'll appreciate the reminder.

Being nine months pregnant during the holidays can be especially trying. Downtown merchants, for example, give you dirty looks every time you walk into their stores because they know that while to the naked eye you may appear to be pregnant, in actuality you're busy stuffing stereos and Nintendo games, as well as several Christmas hams, underneath your coat when nobody is looking.

Actually, I don't mean to whine. At least I get to go to a clean, well-lit hospital staffed by skilled people when the time comes for me to deliver. Mary didn't have that option. Mary, heavy and far from home, couldn't even get a room. When she delivered, it was in the hay of a stable lit by stars. My experience, I'm sure, will be quite different from hers.

Still, I find that I relate to the Christmas story on a deeply personal level this holiday season. That's because it is more than a record of a single birth in Bethlehem a long time ago. It is ultimately a story about the longing that accompanies all births.

Humanity has not always acquitted itself well over the years. History often reads like an endless saga of the evil men do to one another, and there is no rational reason whatsoever to believe that things will change in the future. And yet every time a baby is about to be born, you can almost hear the human race hold its collective breath and say, "Well! Maybe this time we'll get it right." There's hope in that voice.

And there is joy, too.

A Christmas Wish

My boy Philip used to break his leg when he was in kindergarten. Sometimes he'd even do it twice in one day.

I'd be in the middle of doing something when one of the neighbor kids would race into the house yelling, "Ann! Ann! Philip broke his legs! Both of them! He needs you bad."

So I'd go outside and find Philip flat on his back, sticking his broken legs straight up in the air so I could check them easier.

"Well," I'd say after an informal examination, "I think these legs are definitely going to be okay."

Then I'd give him a hug and—miracle of miracles—those legs got better right away.

One night when I was attempting to fix dinner while soothing a frantic baby at the height of the witching hour (5:00 p.m. to 6:00 pm.), Philip's friend Charley came tearing into the kitchen.

"Ann! Philip fell off his bike and broke his leg!"

Frankly, I was not in the mood for this kind of news. "Tell him to come home, and I'll take care of it."

"But he's too far away," said Charley. "He needs you to pick him up."

I held firm and showed Charley our door. Fifteen minutes passed and Philip's friend Jeff showed up.

"Ann, Philip broke his leg. For reals."

The telephone rang. The baby wailed. The spaghetti boiled over. "I'll fix it as soon as he comes home!" I snapped.

Another ten minutes and Michael showed up. "PHILIP'S LEG IS BROKEN! NO LIE!"

Panic pricked my stomach. Maybe his leg really was broken. Maybe he was writhing in pain in the middle of Second Avenue during rush hour, waiting for me while neighbors looked on and said, "We always knew his mother was trash." I grabbed the baby and raced to the car.

I found Philip lying on the ground by his bike, surrounded by a group of buddies.

They were all smiling and laughing and having a swell time be-cause Philip—get this—was telling knock-knock jokes.

"YOUR LEGS ARE NOT BROKEN!" I shouted through my open window. "THEY'RE NOT EVEN SPRAINED!"

Everyone turned around to look at me, and the expression on Philip's face said he knew his goose was seriously cooked unless he came up with a new wrinkle. Fast.

"I know, I know," he said quickly. "I was just kidding about that. It's my *feet* that are broken. Honest, Mom." Then he crawled toward the car on his belly just like GI Joe to convince me.

I came completely unstrung at that point. I tossed the bike *and* Philip into the car and took off doing about 120 mph. When we got home I sent him straight to his room. "And no more faking injuries," I warned.

"But I really was hurt," he called as he limped up the stairs. Then he threw me a glance that almost made me stop breathing. He looked exactly like my brother John when he was six years old.

Suddenly I had a memory. It was Christmas Eve, and John and I were out delivering food gifts to the neighbors. The night was cold and white, and our breath hung like clouds in the frosty air.

"Let's sing," said John as we stamped up and down frozen streets, so we ran through every Christmas carol we knew at the top of our lungs.

By the time we got home, we were hopelessly wound up. John's face was red and his eyes glittered. I felt hot and dizzy and a little sick to my stomach. We kept singing inside, singing and laughing and fi-nally chasing each other through the living room where the adults—grandparents, great-aunts, a collection of neighbors—were eating hors d'oeuvres and watching Lawrence Welk.

Mom collared us. "Settle down." But as soon as she let us go, we were at it again, like toy tops spinning out of control.

This time she removed us bodily into another room. "What is the matter with you two?" She was at her wit's end.

"I—I'm sick," I blurted out.

"Well, then maybe you ought to go to bed!" she snapped.

No, no. I'm not really sick. I'm excited. I'm crazy with happiness be-cause I love snow and cold air on my face and the fire in the fireplace. I love the presents in their wrapping paper and the ornaments on the tree and the music box that plays Silent Night. *I love Christmas, and I especially love you and John, too.*

That's what I wanted to say to her, but I didn't know how, because I was only eight years old. So I said I was sick instead, and she misunderstood, just like I misunderstood about Philip's broken bones.

If I could have one wish granted this holiday season, I would like to be eight all over again, waiting with my brother John for Christmas to come. I would like to eat apples and cookies and hear my old aunts talk about Lawrence Welk and just one more time see my brother's bright believing face. I would like to feel everything I did then in our old living room filled with the smells of fire and pine.

That's what I want for Christmas this and every year.

But I know it won't happen, so instead I would like to remember what it's like to be very young—how easy it is to talk abut physical hurts, how hard it is to turn feelings into words.

The Year My Brothers and I Turned into the Herdmans

*T*his is a true story about the Christmas my brothers and I turned into the Herdmans. The Herdmans, if you'll recall, were the obnoxious siblings in *The Best Christmas Pageants Ever*, by Barbara Robinson. They did stuff like smoke in the bathrooms, blackmail other kids at recess, steal Christmas hams, etc., which naturally made all the neighbors hate them. Well, my brothers and I did not smoke in the bathrooms, blackmail other kids at recess or steal hams, but we still made all the neighbors hate us just the same. Here's how.

It was a typical Christmas Eve at our house which meant that there were lots of relatives hanging around, inhaling vast quantities of food because my family has always been seriously into eating.

"Do you realize that the only thing your family remembers about trips are the meals you ate?" a sister-in-law once said to me.

I just stared at her blankly because, frankly, I didn't get her point.

"Speaking of trips, Ann," my brother, her husband, piped up, "do you remember that breaded shrimp we ate in Winnemucca?"

So, as I was saying, there were plenty of us from the same gene pool sitting around my parents' living room with the old feedbags strapped firmly in place, watching TV, and generally making merry.

When *Bewitched* was over—it was that episode where Samantha takes a kid who doesn't believe in Santa Claus anymore for a quick spin through the North Pole—my dad announced it was time for bed. Of course we (a) wheedled and (b) whined, begging him to let us please please stay up for just a few more minutes, but my father held firm.

"Here you guys," he said slipping his watch from his wrist as he scooted us off to bed. "Wake your mom and me when it's 6:00 a.m. and not a minute before. Okay?"

As was our custom, the kids all slept in the same room on Christmas Eve.

Before he crawled into the top bunk, my brother John looped my father's watch over the bedpost so that he could eyeball it at regular intervals throughout the night. As I pulled the covers over me, I knew that each endless moment until 6:00 a.m. would be the purest agony, not unlike natural childbirth.

For a while we chattered like jays until one by one we finally dropped off to sleep so that visions of sugarplums and other foodstuffs such as stolen hams could dance through our heads.

In the morning John awoke us with a bellow and a yelp. "Oh my gosh. It's ten past six. We slept in!"

Slept in? Slept in? I could hardly believe my ears. There had never been a Christmas we'd slept in. I was beginning to wonder if our parents had spiked our punch with sleeping drugs from the pharmacist down the street who always put his own kids out of commission until noon Christmas Day. We leaped out of our beds, turned on the lights, and raced down the hallway to my parents' bedroom.

"Six o'clock already?" my father mumbled, his hair sticking out like fins from the side of his head. "Geez, I feel like I just went to bed."

"Oh well," yawned my mother, "let's get up. Christmas comes but once a year." So my parents shuffled out of bed and wrapped themselves in robes while we raced off to wake up the grandparents and elderly aunts who were also staying with us, and before you knew it there was a fire in the fireplace, a coffee cake on the table, and a little pile of presents at everybody's feet.

Now here comes the part where we turned into the Herdmans.

As soon as we opened all our presents, my brothers and I started to call our friends who lived up and down the street. We noticed that people were taking an unusually long time to answer the phone, and when they did it was usually the dad who barked THAT EVERY-BODY AT THIS HOUSE IS STILL ASLEEP before hanging up on us. Not long after that we heard a commotion on our front lawn, and when we peered out the window, we saw these very same fathers all dressed in robes and carpet slippers, brandishing pitchforks and torches and screaming at us like the villagers in all those old Franken-stein movies.

"Oh my," said my mother.

As it turned out they were mad at us because I and my brothers—i.e., the Herdmans—had called their houses at 3:30 in the morning. John, who had a hard time with long hands and short hands, had misread the watch. Ten after six was actually 2:30. My father felt like he'd just gone to bed because in point of fact, he had.

I learned some important lessons from this experience. The first lesson is that you should never take a kid's word for it when he tells you it's 6:00 a.m. on Christmas morning. The second is that you should never put my brother John in charge of your watch. And the third is that if by chance you're awakened anyway by a herd of bug-eyed kids so excited they can barely breathe, you should try to respond with grace and good humor, just the way my own parents did.

I wish them and everyone else who greets the season with a brave face a truly joyous Christmas.

Christmas Doll

My four-year-old son wants a doll he once saw on television for Christmas. There are those who would say that this means I am a very successful parent, that I have managed to raise a non-sexist male child who is in touch with the sensitive side of himself—the side that wants to love, to nurture, to take care of a doll, even though he is a little boy.

Actually, he wants the doll because it burps.

I'm not kidding. This doll is called Baby Burpee, and when you hoist it over ye olde shoulder, then slap it on the back, it belches—belches, for petessakes—just like your standard-issue teenage boy in a junior high school cafeteria.

"Now who thought this up?" I asked myself in a state of total shock the first time I saw the commercial. Who really and truly thought we needed more things in this world that burp in public?

Geoffrey, on the other hand, thinks a doll that burps is a swell idea, rating a big ten on the Toys that Make Disgusting Bodily Noises Scale, right up there with whoopie cushions and so forth. Geoffrey, along with his four brothers, is heavily into bodily noises—a guy thing for sure—which is why he wants a doll for Christmas, a doll that burps, thereby leaving all the guys who live in this house on the floor, laughing and snorting hysterically.

Oh well, I tell myself, I suppose there are worse dolls on the market today. Take Tattoodles, for instance. My friend claims she saw this doll complete with its very own tattoo kit advertised in a local circular. And then there's Totally Hair Barbie. Totally Hair Barbie has very, very Big Hair. Serious Hair. Buffalo Hair. Hair Down to There. The Greatest Hair on Earth, just like all that hair you see on Texas drill teams. Totally Hair Barbie makes country western singer Crystal Gale's hairdo look like a very short pixie cut. To tell you the truth, Totally Hair Barbie gives me a serious case of the willies.

Still, I know what it feels like to want a doll. The Christmas I was six years old, I wanted a doll, only I didn't know exactly which one because I hadn't been to the toy store. I hadn't been anywhere, in fact, not since September when I was diagnosed with acute nephritis.

Sometimes I wonder how kids with nephritis are treated today, although since I am (a) lazier than I am (b) curious, I've never bothered to find out. However, in those days—shortly after man discovered fire—they packed you off to bed with a pharmacy full of penicillin and told you not to get out again for months and months.

So there I was, languishing in my bed, all pale and wan, just like some suffering child in a bad Victorian novel. Meanwhile it was December, and outside my window neighborhood kids were building snowmen, making snow angels, tossing snowballs. The last time I'd played with them, the aspens in the foothills behind our house were barely tipped with yellow.

The week before Christmas my parents said they had a surprise for me. They bundled me in blankets and drove me to Salt Lake City where we went to the Cottonwood Mall to look at toys. Dad carried me in his arms so the two of us looked just like Heidi's invalid friend, Clara, and her father, Herr What's-his-face.

I found the doll I wanted.

When Christmas Eve finally came, I said one of those secret kid prayers, wishing with all my heart that I might receive her. I went to bed early that night (no big deal—I was already there), waiting for morning to come, when my parents slipped into my room to listen to Dad's brand new Nat King Cole record. The family's only hi-fi stood right next to my nightstand.

I became increasingly agitated as Nat's honeyed voice filled the air. "You need to leave," I told my parents, who gave me indulgent smiles.

I persisted. "If you don't leave, Santa Claus won't come!" *He won't come and give me my beautiful doll. Just leave. Please.*

"Of course, Santa will come," Dad soothed. I could tell he really wanted to listen to that new record, but in the end Mom made him leave. They kissed me, then shut my door softly behind them.

I received the doll that Christmas, all right, but in retrospect I am a little hazy about her features. Was she big or small? Did her eyes open and shut? Did she burp?

I can't remember.

What I do remember about that Christmas is the look of pleasure on my father's face as he dropped his new record onto the turntable. He was so young then. Much younger than I am now.

So please don't leave, Mom and Dad. Stay with me this Christmas Eve, with the snow lying silver on the ground beneath a wide holiday moon. Stay with me by the fire here and let us listen together to Nat King Cole and Judy Garland and Bing Crosby, too. To carols. To all our half-remembered tunes.

To all the wonderful old songs.